ETHIOPIA TODAY
Ernest W. Luther

In a sophisticated world, the name Ethiopia, which dates from Biblical times, still has for many a strange and exotic ring. There is, of course, a great deal about Ethiopia that is obscure, and while this book may not dispel the impression of strangeness, it will replace the vagueness with facts. Some of the following, for example, may surprise the reader:

The peoples of Ethiopia are almost exclusively Caucasian, and Negroes were formerly hunted down and captured for use as slaves.

The state religion of Ethiopia is Christianity. The Ethiopian Orthodox Church was established in the fourth century A.D., and it is generally accepted by scholars as authentic that two small boys were responsible for the conversion of this part of the world to Christianity.

No adequate surveys have been made of Ethiopia's gold and other minerals, and despite some ten years of drilling for oil and United States investments of $10,000,000, only dry wells have been produced so far.

The Ethiopians speak a total of forty different languages.

Ethiopia's main export crop is coffee, and the national prosperity depends in large part on fluctuations in the world coffee market.

Formerly landlocked, Ethiopia was federated with Eritrea in 1952, thus gaining a seacoast for the first time. Over half the Empire's imports and exports now pass through the ports of Massawa and Assab.

Ethiopia has a new constitution (1955), "a strange composite of monarchical tradition and Western parliamentary concepts."

Almost all efforts to transform Ethiopia into a modern economy can be traced directly to Emperor Haile Selassie. From one point of view, Ethiopia's major problem can be described as how to communicate the Emperor's convictions and ideals to the people.

Here, then, is authentic information on Ethiopia, but the book is not only a source of facts. The author has skillfully marshaled his facts and brought them into perspective. From his six years in Ethiopia (1950–56), he has acquired an intimate acquaintance with the land and the people. His experience and travel as Economist for the State Bank of Ethiopia gave him a unique opportunity also to report on economic, political, and social conditions in the country. The result is a clear and incisive bird's-eye view of present-day Ethiopia.

ETHIOPIA
TODAY

ERNEST W. LUTHER

ERNEST W. LUTHER is at present Monetary and Statistics Adviser to the Bank Melli Iran in Teheran under the sponsorship of the International Co-operation Administration.

STANFORD UNIVERSITY PRESS
STANFORD, CALIFORNIA

LONDON: OXFORD UNIVERSITY PRESS

1958

STANFORD UNIVERSITY PRESS
STANFORD, CALIFORNIA

LONDON: OXFORD UNIVERSITY PRESS

© 1958 BY THE BOARD OF TRUSTEES OF THE
LELAND STANFORD JUNIOR UNIVERSITY

LIBRARY OF CONGRESS CATALOG CARD NUMBER: 58-7842

PRINTED IN THE UNITED STATES OF AMERICA

TO MY WIFE

Anneliese

Preface

The name Ethiopia dates from biblical times. It has always had rather obscure associations, however, and even today, after the publicity given the country by the war with Italy in 1935, some people may find it difficult to locate the area on a map. In the most recent years it has come into renewed prominence as the result of a growing number of foreign contacts, both political and commercial, including the participation of Ethiopian troops in the Korean War and the Emperor of Ethiopia's 1954 visit to Europe and the United States. Much of the publicity given to Ethiopia has been misleading, and it is one of the aims of this book to correct that impression by bringing the relevant facts concerning the country into their proper perspective. Of course, that perspective is still only one man's view (and an economist's at that). A sociologist or theologian might very well offer a different one.

It is difficult to make specific acknowledgment to the many sources from which material for this book has been derived. Some of them will be recognized from the footnotes scattered throughout its pages. Others are acquaintances of mine now living in Ethiopia, so that it would be injudicious to mention their names. But for the most part the book stems from my own experiences during my stay in Ethiopia (1950–56) and from the research I was engaged in while there.

It is hoped that the book will appeal to the general reader as well as to those especially interested in Ethiopian affairs, and that it will prove of some genuine value in helping people to understand an ancient land that is just now beginning to emerge from obscurity.

E.W.L.

Washington, D.C.
March 1958

Contents

ETHIOPIA TODAY

I

Geography and Climate

The Empire of Ethiopia is situated in the horn of East Africa just above the equator. It has an area (including Eritrea) of roughly 450,000 square miles and a population variously estimated at between ten and twenty million. It is bounded on the west and northwest by the Sudan, on the north by the Red Sea, on the east and southeast by French, British, and Italian Somaliland, respectively, and on the south by Kenya. Formerly completely landlocked, it acquired a seacoast when it was joined with Eritrea under a unique federal arrangement by United Nations action in 1952.

Ethiopia is a country of great diversity, in its topography, in its climate, and in its peoples, languages, and customs. It is fashioned of a conglomeration of widely divergent and occasionally hostile races and tribes, politically united within their present borders only since the beginning of the twentieth century. One writer has called it a land in which "the past lies heavy, very remote, actual and indecipherable."[1] The country seems "masked behind her capital,"[2] for semimodern Addis Ababa is scarcely representative of Ethiopia. Outside of the capital and the few large towns life goes on much as it always has for centuries, slowly, ponderously, with the mass of the people hardly aware even of their own existence as a constituent element in a larger and more unified whole.

Ethiopia has been virtually isolated from Western civilization until

[1] David Mathew, *Ethiopia* (London, 1947), p. 5.
[2] *Ibid.*

very recent times. A key factor in this isolation has been her immensely difficult terrain, cleft in numerous places by canyons of great depth, which often rendered communications impossible, especially in the period of the heavy rains. These natural obstacles, together with the aloofness and sometimes open hostility of the people, preserved the country from foreign penetration for many years, except for occasional missionaries and private travelers. Under these conditions it is indeed odd, as Buxton points out, that the name of Ethiopia should have been known to Europe for centuries while knowledge of most of the rest of Africa was still shrouded in ignorance.[3]

The country may be described as consisting in the main of a huge tableland or plateau, thousands of feet in height, and divided into two sections by the great Rift Valley, running northeast from central Kenya to the Red Sea. The plateau rises abruptly from the surrounding semidesert areas on almost all sides, in a series of steep slopes or escarpments that in places have a sheer drop of several thousand feet. The western half of this tableland inclines slightly toward the Sudan, and most of the rivers run in that direction; the eastern part is tilted toward the Indian Ocean. The plateau country is rent in many places by deep valleys and enormous fissures, formed in the course of milleniums both by tectonic movements and by erosion, the result of the heavy summer rainfall running off from the high plateau to the adjacent lowlands in torrential streams. The same process of erosion, unchecked even today, has created or left standing, where the surrounding soil has been washed away, hills resembling truncated cones of weird shape and design. These *ambas,* as they are called, have sometimes played an important role in Ethiopian history, serving as prisons or sheltering monasteries or providing a well-nigh impregnable refuge for kings and their following in time of invasion. Their large, level tops permitted the growing of crops or the herding of cattle, thus affording a complete self-sufficiency to the inhabitants, while their steep slopes were easily defensible. In addition to the *ambas,* true mountain ranges also exist, mainly to the east and southeast of Lake Tana, but also on the eastern plateau across the Rift Valley south-southeast of

[3] David Buxton, *Travels in Ethiopia* (London, 1949), p. 22.

the capital. Some of the peaks reach heights of 14,000 and even 15,000 feet; the highest, Ras Dashan in the Semien Mountains northeast of Lake Tana, is stated to be approximately 15,160 feet high.

Geologists ascribe the formation of the country to a series of eruptions during the Mesozoic era, when the eastern part of Africa was raised far above the level of the sea in a broad, flat arch. Later, the subsidence of the earth's crust that created the Indian Ocean caused the eastern part of this arch to give way, forming the great African rift. This rift, and the two sections of the Ethiopian plateau which it bifurcates, are the dominant geographic features of the country.

The Rift Valley in its lower part holds a chain of lakes. Further along it becomes the valley of the Awash River, the only major stream of the central plateau to flow eastward. Still further along it broadens out into a gigantic fan as it opens onto the Danakil plains, a desert area inhabited by semisavage nomads whose allegiance to the government at Addis Ababa is still only of the loosest kind. In general, the valley floor is some 2,000–3,000 feet below the crest of the escarpments that form the walls. It extends from an elevation of approximately 6,000 feet north of Lake Zwai (the northernmost of the chain of lakes) to below 2,000 feet above sea level in the neighborhood of Lake Stefanie near the southern border. Its average width is about thirty miles to the point where it opens onto the Danakil plains.

The central highlands are generally tilted westwards, but in places the dip is from north to south, or vice versa. In the north elevations of 8,000–9,000 feet are fairly common; in the south the plateau rarely exceeds 6,500 feet. The south has more open tableland and fewer lofty peaks than the north, but the general character of the two regions is the same—a much broken and highly dissected rolling plateau.

The eastern escarpment of the northern highlands rises sheer above the Red Sea plains for many thousands of feet, and approaches to the plateau from these plains are therefore few and difficult. The escarpment continues southward to the valley of the Awash, which lies some 3,000 feet lower and forms a gateway to the plateau. At this point the escarpment turns southwest to become the western wall of the Rift Valley. It becomes progressively less high and steep as one follows it in the direction of the Kenya border and Lake Rudolph.

In the west the escarpment is not as pronounced as in the east and drops somewhat more gradually to the Sudan plains in a series of terrace-like descents. It is considerably more broken here, often by rivers draining to the Nile Valley. In places it is ill-defined and very broken, falling gradually to the western desert.

The eastern plateau exhibits many of the same general characteristics as the western or central plateau, but it is not a uniformly elevated tableland. From its maximum altitude in the north it descends southeastwards as a gigantic and regular plain, finally becoming a large, low, semiarid belt parallel to the coast of the Indian Ocean. The valleys of the eastern plateau run in the direction of the maximum slope and are not as deep as those of the central highlands. The plateau is well wooded in its middle, with open, grassy glades alternating with patches of forest; further south it gradually loses this appearance and becomes a dry, hot area where only thornbush will grow.

The Danakil plains, into which the Rift Valley opens, form the eastern frontiers of the Empire. They extend all along the coast to the northernmost part of Eritrea, where they are known as the Red Sea plains. This is a formidable and inhospitable desert area, in some places below sea level, sloping to the north and east. It is here that the Awash River empties into a small chain of salt lakes on the French Somaliland border and thus never reaches the sea. To the north lies the Kobar Depression, a saline below-sea-level area some hundred miles long and forty miles wide, where commercial extraction of salt is now in progress. East of this zone of depression there is a range of volcanic coastal mountains increasing in height toward the south and reaching an altitude of 6,700 feet near Assab on the Red Sea. With the exception of the narrow coastal plains the whole region drains inland, most of the streams losing themselves in the Kobar Depression or in the lakes that terminate the Awash.

Owing to Ethiopia's generally high elevation, its climate is temperate despite the proximity of the whole area to the equator. The average annual temperature of the highlands is sixty to sixty-five degrees Fahrenheit, and there is but little variation from month to month. Frost is sometimes encountered, but never snow, and even at midday the warmth of the sun is not oppressive. For the most part the climate of the highlands is very agreeable and uniform. One has only to descend several thousand feet, however, to come upon totally different conditions. Regions of subtropical climate are to be found in numerous places, even in the heart of the highlands, where these are dissected by deep river valleys, such as the valley of the Blue Nile. In these deep valleys, as well as in the lowlands and semidesert areas surrounding the plateau on almost all sides, not only the temperature but the flora and fauna are strikingly different. These rapid and extreme changes of climate are one of the major geographical characteristics of Ethiopia as it presents itself to the traveler, and are of considerable economic importance.

Ethiopians themselves apply the terms *quolla, woina dega,* and *dega* to the climatic zones of their country, corresponding roughly to hot, temperate, and cold. These terms are sometimes also applied to isolated pockets of one type of climate within a larger surrounding zone of another kind. There seem to be no generally agreed limiting elevations in defining the three types of zone; roughly speaking, the first term applies to the desert and semiarid lowlands, the second to the plateau country, and the last to the mountain areas above 8,000 feet.

Ethiopia's climate may be divided into two seasons, the dry and the wet. The wet or rainy season lasts from about mid-June through September in the central plateau region, but may be considerably extended in the southeast, south, and southwest. The dry season follows, and is interrupted only once, during February or March, when the "little rains" fall, before the onset of the main rainy season or "big rains" in June. Although no proven explanation has yet been given for this pattern, one theory has it that the regularity of the rains and their concentration at one or two periods of the year is attributable to the monsoon winds that blow over the Indian Ocean in a westerly direction, shifting regularly from north to south. These winds pick up moisture from the Indian Ocean and release it on striking the highlands of Ethiopia. After about four months they have shifted far enough to the north to be blowing over the Arabian desert, and they then become dry. On their way south again they cause the "little rains," a period of sporadic, though sometimes very heavy, rainfall.

The wet and dry seasons are not sharply defined and are not identical for all parts of the country, or even for the same region from one year to another.

Ethiopia's rainfall is, in general, adequate for agriculture, except in the semiarid and desert regions. The west and southwest high plateau country has the greatest precipitation, sixty to seventy inches annually. The Chercher plateau region in the eastern highlands is another zone of high precipitation, and the central plateau north of the capital another. Fifty to sixty inches annually fall in these areas. The amount of rainfall increases toward the southwest, but tapers off in the direction of the southern slopes and the Kenya border. The Rift Valley, the Danakil plains, and the Ogaden semidesert are areas of little precipitation (twenty inches or less), and support a highly nomadic and pastoral life. The Sudan slopes, however, although very low and hot, receive in the southwest a substantial amount of rain, and are very rich in tropical vegetation. In other subtropical areas the vegetation is chiefly thornbush. In the humid southwest, where the precipitation is fairly evenly distributed throughout a large part of the year, there are areas of dense forest.

Hail causes frequent damage to crops in the high plateau regions. Wind is also responsible for some crop damage, especially during the rains. A rather strong wind prevails during much of the dry season and in the period of the little rains. This, together with the intense sunlight, causes a rapid rate of free water evaporation and loss of soil moisture. Also contributing to this result is the nature of the soil itself, which in most parts of the country is volcanic in origin. It has a crumb structure which permits rapid intake of water, but from which free water is also lost very quickly. Often, following a heavy rain during the night, a few hours of sunshine suffice to dry the soil so that it can be tilled.

Ethiopia has numerous rivers, but many of them are shallow and precipitous and are dry for the greater part of the year. Others are perennial. Waterfalls are frequent, and there are a number of attractive potential sites for the production of hydroelectric power. None of the rivers is navigable except the Baro, and this only for a short distance inland to Gambeila in the period of the heavy rains.

The virtual absence of navigable waterways is a great handicap to transportation in a country already so handicapped in this respect by its mountainous terrain. In the central highlands the main river systems are the Takazze in the north, the Abbai or Blue Nile in the center, and the Baro in the south. The Blue Nile originates in Lake Tana, the country's largest lake, and flows through a tremendous gorge (reminiscent of the Grand Canyon) to unite, eventually, with the White Nile in the Sudan, thus forming the main body of the Nile. These three river systems, according to one estimate,[4] carry off roughly 80 per cent of the entire drainage of the country. The remainder is carried off largely by the Barka, which runs north and occasionally reaches the Red Sea near Suakin in the Sudan; by the Webi Shebeli and the Juba, which flow southeast through the eastern plateau (though only the latter reaches the sea); and by the Omo, flowing south to Lake Rudolph.

Only about 7 per cent of the country is forested. The chief forest regions are in the west and southwest and in the highlands of Chercher and Arussi southeast of the capital; they are about evenly divided between closed, high forest and open forest alternating with patches of grassland. The scarcity of forest is due to the insufficiency or uneven annual distribution of rain in most areas; even in regions of relatively high precipitation savannahs predominate, because of the concentration of the rain in three or four months of the year. Another reason for the scarcity of forest is the centuries-old practice of unrestricted denudation of forested areas, especially in the northern highlands, with no attempt at reforestation. Before the establishment of a permanent capital at Addis Ababa some seventy-five years ago it was the custom of Ethiopian emperors and their retinue to move about from place to place as the timber resources became exhausted. No action has yet been taken by the Ethiopian government to conserve the small and scattered forest areas remaining.

The trees of Ethiopia have not all been botanically defined, but over a hundred species have thus far been recorded. Most are mi-

---

[4] *Guide Book of Ethiopia* (Addis Ababa Chamber of Commerce, 1954), p. 116.

nutely to finely porous, but coarsely porous very light woods are also to be found. Around the capital itself eucalyptus abounds, but this is not indigenous. There have to date been no extensive lumbering operations for export, partly because the limited road network leaves most of the forest areas relatively inaccessible.

Approximately 30 per cent of the country's land area is pastoral, 9 per cent arable, 22 per cent bush and thornbush, and the rest—almost one-third—desert or otherwise unproductive.[5]

Some arable land is to be found in all save the outright desert areas, but the heaviest concentration is in the northern highlands. Other arable areas include parts of the southern and southeastern slopes, and the Rift Valley along the Awash River. Some experts maintain that the arable land is being used too heavily, and with little concern for conservation. Erosion is plainly extreme in many areas. Methods of agriculture are primitive. These and other considerations relating to land use will be discussed in detail in Chapter VI.

[5] These figures are estimates of the Food and Agriculture Organization of the United Nations (FAO).

II

History

The history of the diverse peoples who inhabit this rugged country is long and obscure. No attempt will be made here to trace it completely.[1] The aim of the following review is merely to acquaint the general reader with some of the more important events in Ethiopia's past and so to provide a sufficient background against which current events and institutions may be seen in their proper perspective.

Most authorities seem to agree that the Ethiopian people had their origin as the result of an influx of Semitic tribes from southern Arabia to the Abyssinian highlands sometime in the first millennium B.C. The migrants conquered, assimilated, and absorbed by intermarriage the basically Hamitic peoples they found there, who in turn, it is thought, had much earlier displaced a predominantly Negro culture. The Semitic-Hamitic descendants of the early invaders eventually spread southward, but the degree of assimilation they were able to achieve with the inhabitants of the regions infiltrated by these secondary migrations was never complete, and there remain to this day scattered enclaves of these bypassed groups, termed *Agau* by the Ethiopians, who have largely preserved their Hamitic speech and pagan religion. For the most part, however, the migrants from Arabia succeeded in imposing on the peoples they conquered their own Semitic tongues and culture; their descendants comprise the ancient nucleus of the

[1] For a good, yet short, account see A. H. M. Jones and Elizabeth Monroe, *A History of Abyssinia* (London, 1935). Unfortunately, no satisfactory history of the most recent period is available.

Abyssinian people. (The term *Ethiopians* came to be applied to these people only at a much later date. The classical geographical position of Ethiopia was not in the Abyssinian highlands at all, but in the middle and lower Nile Valley, then called Cush or Nubia.)

Beginning in the fourth century Somali tribes, who had been converted to Islam, began to invade the highlands. In the sixteenth century began the Galla migrations into Ethiopia. These continued for several hundred years, and in the course of time the Gallas, whose original home is uncertain, succeeded in occupying vast tracts of the southern highlands. Still later, toward the end of the nineteenth century, additional "foreign" races and tribes, over which the old Ethiopian kings had never ruled, came to be incorporated into the Empire as a result of the territorial conquests of the Emperor Menelik II.

The original Semitic-Hamitic peoples of the north, descendants of the migrants from Arabia, gradually achieved political consolidation in the Kingdom of Aksum. This kingdom seems to have flourished from at least the first century A.D. to the seventh. Its civilization appears to have been of quite a high order, judging from the numerous coins, monuments, inscriptions, and broken relics that have been found by archaeologists in this region. The kings of Aksum openly proclaimed their paganism—an interesting and sufficient refutation, incidentally, of the famous legend, still current in Ethiopia, to the effect that the present dynasty is descended from a union between King Solomon and the Queen of Sheba, the latter identified with Makeda, Queen of Ethiopia. The legend originated, it is thought, in the thirteenth century upon the restoration of the "Solomonian" line following the brief rule of the Zagwe dynasty, in order to give the new rulers the sanction of divine authority.

The kings of Aksum wielded considerable power in their day and ranged far afield, even as far as southern Arabia, which they raided and held for a time. But since most of their conquests did not have settlement or annexation as their goal, it is difficult to know what were the political boundaries of this ancient kingdom and how far the sovereignty of its kings extended. A fair guess is that the Kingdom of Aksum was probably limited to the regions of modern Eritrea and Tigre.

In the fourth century A.D. the Kingdom of Aksum was converted to Christianity under conditions which may be described as highly romantic but are nevertheless generally accepted by scholars as authentic. A philosopher of Tyre, on a sea voyage with two small boys whom he was educating, happened to stop at a port on the East African coast. His ship was boarded and all the pasengers and crew were murdered except the two small boys, who had found favor with the local king. These boys were raised and cared for by the king, and were later given posts of trust and responsibility in his kingdom. In time they succeeded in converting the king and his people to their own faith, Christianity. One of them, Frumentius by name, traveled at maturity to Alexandria, where he was consecrated by a bishop of the Egyptian Coptic Church and sent back among the Abyssinians to continue his work of conversion. Thus the connection of the Ethiopian Orthodox Church with the Church of Alexandria was first established, a connection that remained essentially unaltered down almost to the present day. After centuries of effort the Ethiopian Church finally succeeded in 1948 in obtaining the consent of Alexandria to become autocephalous.

The Kingdom of Aksum fell into obscurity following the rise of Islam in the seventh century A.D., and little more is heard of the country until the coming of the Portuguese in the sixteenth. During these "centuries of historical night,"[2] Ethiopia underwent an eclipse such as few countries have ever known. Only at rare intervals was the curtain lifted to shed some light on what was happening within its borders. From the little evidence available it is clear that the Aksumite civilization crumbled and that nothing comparable took its place. There are no further records of historical achievement, no monuments, coins, or relics dating from a later period to indicate that a cultural continuity had been maintained. It may be conjectured that during this long period the already assimilated people of the northern highlands engaged in new migrations to the south, coming in contact with additional Hamitic groups and thereby further diluting the

[2] J. B. Coulbeaux, *Histoire politique et religieuse de l'Abyssinie* (Paris, 1929), I, 203.

"original" stock. It was probably a period in which hundreds of minor wars were fought as a result of this southward expansion, bringing in their train a large number of conversions to the Christian faith. Ethiopia may have had its own "crusades."

In the twelfth century a new dynasty, the Zagwe, came to power. It claimed descent from Moses and ruled for 133 years, according to Ethiopian chroniclers, before the "Solomonian" line was restored about 1270 in the person of Yekuno Amlak. One of the Zagwe kings, Lalibela, is credited with the construction of a number of monolithic churches, hewn from solid rock, which—with the single exception of the Gondarene castles of Fasilidas in the sixteenth century—constitute the only Ethiopian architectural achievements comparable to those of ancient Aksum up to the present day. These churches still stand, though in poor condition, in the old province of Lasta, accessible only by mule. The largest, the Church of the Redeemer of the World, measures 100 by 75 feet, with an additional row of external pillars extending to the full height of the edifice. Inside there are five aisles and twenty-eight pillars, delicately worked, the whole attesting to the architects' ingenuity and the craftsmen's skill.[3]

The "Solomonian" restoration coincided with, or more likely stimulated, a revival of literary activity, which up to that period had been extremely light. It was in this period that the sacred *Kebra Negast* ("Glory of Kings") was committed to writing. Some Arabic and Coptic works were translated into Ge'ez, the classical and liturgical language of Ethiopia, and a number of hagiographical books were written. It is not clear whether the New Testament was first translated into Ge'ez at this time or much earlier by Frumentius at the time of the conversion to Christianity.

In the fourteenth and fifteenth centuries many campaigns were fought by the country's monarchs against the tide of Islam swelling and surging about the base of the Abyssinian mountain fortress. It appears that conclusive victories were seldom won by either side, but that each succeeded at times in penetrating deep into the other's terri-

[3] There is some doubt whether both the Gondarene castles and the churches of Lalibela are, in fact, indigenous creations.

tory. The Moslems were at one time, even before the destructive invasions of Muhammed Grañ in the sixteenth century, reported to have overrun the whole of northern Ethiopia. As a result of these wars the Abyssinian kings gradually lost control of northern Tigre and the coastal areas.

The story of a Christian monarch of the East struggling against the Moslems eventually reached Europe, where it was rumored that this ruler was the legendary Prester John of the Indies. The Portuguese were particularly interested in securing the aid of such an ally in the fight against Islam, and after several abortive attempts succeeded in 1520 in establishing an embassy in Ethiopia, whose ruler they had somehow identified with Prester John. This was the first such contact in the history of Ethiopia. The chaplain of this embassy, Father Francisco Alvarez, recorded the significant events of his six years' stay there in his well-known "Narrative of the Portuguese Embassy to Abyssinia, 1520–27." This book gives a wealth of information on what the country was like before the Moslem invasions of the sixteenth century, when most of its churches and monasteries were sacked and burned. Published in 1540, it at long last dispelled Europe's ignorance of this strange and distant land.

With the coming of the Portuguese the period of Ethiopia's isolation from civilization may be said to have ended. From here on the accounts of historians, missionaries, and adventurers become steadily more numerous. Alvarez states that he was questioned closely and intensively concerning church matters. At this time the doctrinal divergence between the Abyssinian and the Roman churches regarding the single or dual nature of Christ had not yet been disclosed. This was later to become part cause of the bitter antagonism between the two faiths and a factor in the expulsion of the Jesuits from Ethiopia.

The Portuguese mission left Abyssinia in 1527. The Moslems had meanwhile become aware of the danger of this affiliation between two Christian nations, and they launched a violent and strong attack upon the country shortly after the embassy's departure. The invading armies, possessing the advantage of firearms and commanded by an able general, Muhammed Grañ, succeeded in overrunning the whole

of Ethiopia, burning and looting the monasteries and putting all
monks to the sword.

Their occupation of Abyssinia lasted some sixteen years. The
emperor, who had taken refuge on an *amba,* managed to smuggle
out an appeal for help to the Portuguese, who replied by landing a
corps of matchlockmen on the coast at Massawa in 1541 and march-
ing inland. The Moslems, meanwhile, had obtained strong rein-
forcements from the Turks, and with this force they attacked and
nearly wiped out the Portuguese. Here the story becomes exciting
and heroic. The armies of Grañ retired, believing the dispersed and
surviving Portuguese to present no danger, and Grañ dismissed his
borrowed corps of riflemen. Although their leader had been killed in
the overwhelming Moslem attack, the soldiers of Portugal managed
to regroup and to restock with hidden weapons. One of their number, a chemist, made gunpowder from local materials. Then, strengthened by a sizable force of Abyssinian warriors, the Portuguese swept
down upon the place where Grañ was unsuspectingly encamped.
The Moslems were taken completely by surprise; Grañ was killed
and his followers routed. The Abyssinians thereafter recovered all the
territory that had been lost to the enemy, and the Moslems never
again bcame a serious threat to their security.

With the decline of Moslem power, however, another threat to the
kingdom began to appear in the form of migrations towards the
highlands of hundreds of thousands of pagan Galla tribesmen from
the southeast. These people, of Hamitic stock, pressed into the
vacuum created by the withdrawal of Grañ's forces, and might have
succeeded in eventually establishing themselves as the dominant political power of the country had a greater unity prevailed among
them. But the Gallas have always fought as readily among themselves
as against their enemies. The upshot of their invasions was merely
that they ushered in some three hundred years of intermittent fighting, confusion, and, ultimately, political chaos, at the end of which
period no fewer than six different men were reigning in various parts
of the country, each claiming to be Emperor.

The Roman Catholic Church contributed to the general confusion when Jesuit missionaries entered the country shortly after the

Moslem defeat in an attempt to convert its rulers to their particular
brand of Christianity. The extreme tactlessness and obdurateness of
one of their number, a monk named Mendez, estranged not only the
Ethiopian clergy but the laity as well, and so embittered the relationship between the Ethiopian and the Roman churches that the Emperor Susenyos, whom the Jesuits had managed to convert, was
forced to abandon his policy of attempted conciliation and to abdi-
cate. His successor, Fasilidas (1632–67), immediately acted to banish
the troublemakers from the Empire and to suppress their teachings.
Rome made several subsequent efforts, which continued for more
than a century, to send missionaries, but those who persisted in the
attempt to enter the country were either stoned to death or otherwise
executed by the Ethiopians.

The Jesuit episode had given a sharp stimulus to religious con-
troversy, which continued to rage for many years amid general civil
war and anarchy. We have a good account of the tribulations of this
period, during which the Abyssinian Empire reached its lowest level
since the dissolution of the Aksumite kingdom, from the Scottish
traveler, James Bruce, who visited the country in 1769 and remained
there several years. At length he could stand it no longer, so vicious
and constant was the bloodletting, and he tells us in his five-volume
work, *Travels to Discover the Source of the Nile,* that he "at last
scarce ever went out, and nothing occupied my thoughts but how to
escape from this bloody country."

Out of this chaotic state of affairs there eventually emerged a
strong man, a robber baron named Kassa, who had built up a considerable private following and who successfully contrived to have
himself crowned Emperor in the year 1855. His throne name was
Theodore, and with his reign the history of contemporary Ethiopia
may be said to begin. Although warfare was still almost continuous,
he attempted to initiate a series of administrative, social, and religious
reforms which had no chance of succeeding but were notable as being
the first attempts of this kind in the history of Ethiopia. He was also
a religious man, yet thoroughly intolerant of both Islam and Roman
Catholicism. His character showed many contradictions, foreshadow-
ing the madness which later overtook him. On the one hand, he was

kind to slaves, sometimes buying them merely to free them from the Moslem traders; on the other, he engaged in the most savage cruelties against those of his own people who displeased him. The enmity he thus incurred among them helped to prepare the way for his own downfall.

This came in 1868. Prey to a growing megalomania, he had imprisoned the British Consul and several other Europeans in retaliation for a supposed snub arising from the British Foreign Office's negligence in replying to a communication he had sent to Queen Victoria. The British government responded to this high-handed act by dispatching a rescue expedition. This force, under the command of Sir Robert Napier, landed near Massawa in 1867 and marched inland, sped on its way by the willing collaboration of the natives who had suffered Theodore's oppression. Theodore's army was met and defeated at Arogee, near Magdala, on April 10, 1868. Unwilling to be taken alive, the Emperor shot himself as the British approached.

Since the object of Napier's expedition was merely the rescue of the European captives, the British forces promptly withdrew when this had been accomplished, taking with them, however, Theodore's crown, the sacred *Kebra Negast* (both subsequently restored), and several other mementos.

The suicide of Theodore gave rise to a renewed period of struggle and confusion, out of which the Ras of Tigre finally emerged triumphant.[4] He was crowned as John IV in 1872. During his reign the European powers began to press seriously against Abyssinia, thanks in large part to the opening of the Suez Canal in 1869, which had laid bare the whole East African coast. Egypt entered the contest, too, seizing the Eritrean coast from Turkey, and reaching as far inland as Harar, an ancient Moslem town now well within the borders of Ethiopia; but these Egyptian conquests soon had to be abandoned, when the Mahdist revolt threatened much nearer home. In 1869 a private Italian company bought the Red Sea port of Assab from a local sultan, and with this Italy made her entry onto the Abyssinian

---

[4] *Ras* is a title of military origin meaning "head," but perhaps better translated as "marshal."

stage. The port was bought out from private control by the Italian government in 1882. In 1885 Italy occupied the port of Massawa, some 275 miles to the north, and she was subsequently encouraged by Great Britain to extend her hegemony inland. Italian attempts in this direction led to a serious defeat at Dogali in 1887, when a small Italian force was almost annihilated by an overwhelming Abyssinian attack. This caused the Italians to try different tactics, namely, direct negotiation with a rival of the Emperor John, King Menelik II, who had become a powerful figure in his own right by his southern and western conquests while John was occupied in the east. They hoped to play him off against John by promising to help him become Emperor in return for his aid. Menelik accepted their gifts of arms and munitions but did nothing. A year later the Emperor John was killed in battle against the Mahdi and his forces routed.

Menelik had no serious rival to the throne and became Emperor the same year (1889). Italy immediately signed with him the Treaty of Ucciali, by which she thought to have obtained a virtual protectorate over Abyssinia. For the Italian text stated that Menelik "consents to avail himself of the Italian Government for any negotiations which he may enter into with other powers or governments." However, the Amharic text, the only one signed, stated only—or so it was claimed—that the Emperor might use the Italians if he so desired. The dispute over this point of the treaty was the first serious rift in Italo-Ethiopian relations, which were to dominate Abyssinian history for the next fifty years. The Italians, meanwhile, consolidated their coastal and inland positions in the north, formally giving the area the name Eritrea in 1890. This, of course, further angered Menelik. Italy sought to appease him by presenting him with additional quantities of arms and munitions. Menelik accepted the presents, but nevertheless denounced the Treaty of Ucciali.

Italian encroachments continued, and with the danger in the north growing ever greater, an Italo-Abyssinian clash became inevitable. Menelik, for once rallying to his support even his rivals and local enemies, marched against the Italian forces and met and defeated them in a major battle at Adowa, then the capital of Tigre, in 1896. The victory is still celebrated yearly as a national holiday in Ethiopia.

The Italians never forgot and never forgave this defeat. As a result of Adowa, Ethiopia for the first time won the respect of the great powers, who now felt obliged to negotiate with her on a basis of mutual equality and independence.[5]

Following Adowa, Menelik experienced a respite from foreign intervention and used it to extend and to consolidate his own territorial holdings. He added thousands of square miles to the Empire by military conquest, largely in the southeast, south, and west, and between 1897 and 1908 succeeded in delimiting the borders of the country by agreement with the European powers substantially as they exist today.[6] He was a strong ruler, and alive to the fact that the country had to advance along the path of modernization if it was not to fall prey to eventual foreign aggrandizement. To this end he began negotiations with the French for a railway to be built from Djibouti, coastal port of French Somaliland, to Addis Ababa, the modern capital founded by him in 1883. The first roads, the first telephone, the first electric lights, the first government school, and the first postal service in Ethiopia were also established during his reign and as the result of his initiative. Unfortunately, his health began to deteriorate shortly after the turn of the century, and with this development the bitter internal, as well as foreign, struggle for power and influence in Ethiopia was resumed. He died in 1913, having been a sick man and a paralytic for years.

During his decline the European powers sought to safeguard their interests in Ethiopia by the tripartite treaty of 1906 (England, France, Italy), in which they affirmed their desire to maintain the country's independence but agreed, in the event of its disintegration, to recognize each other's special spheres of influence. These were, for England, the Lake Tana area and the Blue Nile basin, for France the railway to Djibouti, and for Italy a strip of land across Ethiopian

[5] Ethiopia's failure to press claims to Eritrea in the peace treaty with Italy of October 1896 is an interesting commentary on her subsequent efforts—notably during the post-World War II negotiations to determine the political future of Eritrea—to impress the world with her rights to this territory.

[6] The changes due to Ethiopian-Eritrean federation (1952) excepted.

territory connecting her two colonies of Italian Somaliland and Eritrea. Menelik, of course, protested, thanking the three governments for their desire to maintain Ethiopia's independence, but letting them know that he considered this agreement as in no way limiting his sovereign rights.

With Menelik's firm hand removed from the tiller, the Ethiopian ship of state floundered badly. For a while near-anarchy and corruption flourished. Menelik's seventeen-year-old grandson and successor Lidj Yasu, a wild and irresponsible youth with leanings toward Islam, reigned only briefly. He was ousted in 1916 by the chiefs and notables of Shoa,[7] who raised an army against him while he was away from the capital, and was promptly excommunicated by the Abuna, the Ethiopian Archbishop, who had previously released the chiefs from their oath of allegiance to him. Lidj Yasu fled to the country of the Danakil, but in 1921 he was captured, bound in golden chains, and entrusted for safekeeping to Ras Kassa, a relative of the present Emperor, Haile Selassie (then known as Ras Tafari).

On the deposition of Lidj Yasu, Zauditu, a daughter of Menelik, was crowned Empress, with the young Ras Tafari designated as regent and heir to the throne. For ten years a bitter struggle of power went on between these two and a third leading personality, the aged War Minister, Fitaurari Habte Giorguis. Habte Giorguis died in 1926, leaving Ras Tafari and the Empress to fight it out alone. Tafari showed the greater skill in these maneuvers. In 1928, when it became obvious that the political center of gravity had shifted strongly in his favor, he forced the Empress to bestow upon him the title of Negus (King). Two years later Zauditu died, and on November 2 of the same year, 1930, Tafari was crowned Emperor amid great ceremony and in the presence of many foreign diplomatic emissaries and notables. He took the throne name of Haile Selassie ("Power of the Trinity"), claiming unbroken descent from the dynasty of Menelik I, supposedly the son of King Solomon and the Queen of Sheba.

Haile Selassie, even before his coronation, had demonstrated a

[7] The capital province of the Empire.

distinctly modern mentality that was in striking contrast with the heavy-footed tradition-mindedness of most of his countrymen. As Ras Tafari he had been active in foreign affairs: he sought and obtained Ethiopia's admission to the League of Nations in 1923, visited Europe in 1925, and concluded a twenty-year "Treaty of Friendship" with Italy in 1928. In 1929 he engaged a Belgian military mission to train the Imperial Guard. The next year he negotiated with the National Bank of Egypt for the purchase of its subsidiary, the Bank of Abyssinia; concurred in a Sudanese-sponsored American engineering survey of Lake Tana; and signed an arms traffic act with Britain, France, and Italy to regularize the importation of arms and munitions into the Empire.

After his coronation the tempo of modernization increased. A constitution, the first in the history of the country, was drawn up and promulgated in 1931, establishing a rudimentary parliament and in other ways setting at least a theoretical limit to the Emperor's hitherto absolute power. Foreign advisers were engaged and new ministries were created. Additional schools were opened. Some administrative reforms were begun, and a new antislavery law was decreed. This law did not finally eliminate the practice of slavery, but it was a powerful step in that direction.[8]

This promising start was violently interrupted when the Wal Wal incident late in 1934 exploded into open war between Italy and Ethiopia the following year. The dispute arose over the question of whether certain territories near the Italian Somaliland–Ethiopian border belonged to Italy or to Ethiopia. Existing boundary treaties showed that they were apparently well within Ethiopia's borders, but Italy had occupied them for some time without drawing a protest. With feeling running high on both sides, a skirmish took place on December 5, 1934, at Wal Wal, in the disputed area, where the Italians had constructed military outposts.

Although each disputant accused the other, it soon became evident that Italy, not Ethiopia, was the intransigent party. The case

[8] The practice of slavery in Ethiopia was still widespread before 1935, despite sporadic attempts since the reign of John IV to stamp it out.

was placed before the League of Nations, of which both countries were members, but this body failed to act to check Italy's obviously aggressive intentions. With this failure, as the Emperor later warned the nations in a moving address at Geneva, the threat of a second world war was greatly increased.

Italian forces began to mass in the Italian colonies of Eritrea and Italian Somaliland, and a combined attack from both directions was launched on October 3, 1935. In about seven months it was all over. The Ethiopian troops, though fighting bravely, were no match for the modern, mechanized forces of Mussolini. The Emperor fled the capital on May 3, 1936, two days before the Italians entered it. He boarded a British cruiser at Djibouti which took him to Palestine, whence, after a brief rest, he continued to England and political asylum.

There the history of this independent East African kingdom might have ended, had not Italy become embroiled in World War II with the Allies. The events of Italy's five-year occupation of Ethiopia will not be retold here, except as they may be referred to later in dealing with the economic development of the Empire. Apparently the occupation was never so complete that the harassing guerilla warfare of isolated Ethiopian patriot bands could be ignored. One of these patriot leaders who held out until the Emperor's return in 1941, Abebe Aragai, was subsequently honored with the title of Ras. He is now Ethiopian Minister of War.

The facts of recent history will be readily recalled to mind. British and Commonwealth forces entered Ethiopia from the Sudan in 1940-41, and in six months of actual fighting had wrested the country from the Italians. Patriot forces, forewarned of the impending liberation attempt, gave valuable assistance. By April 1941, Addis Ababa had fallen, and on May 5, five years to the day after the Italian forces had taken the city, the Emperor re-entered his capital. The campaign was now virtually ended. "Mopping-up" operations continued for some months more, and in January of the following year the last remaining Italian stronghold, at Gondar, surrendered. Mussolini's East African Empire lay shattered, and Ethiopia, the first of the victims of aggression, became the first to be freed.

In the initial years of the restoration Ethiopia was governed by mutual agreement with the British, whose military strategists wanted to be assured of a safe land route across Africa to the Red Sea. The political relationship established between Ethiopia and Britain at this time was defined by special agreements between the two countries in 1942 and 1944. The story of how Ethiopia has developed politically, economically, and socially since it was given a new lease on life by the power of British arms will constitute the main theme of this book, to be elaborated in the following chapters.

III

Society, Religion, and Culture

We have seen that Ethiopian civilization very probably had its origins in a Semitic-Hamitic conflux sometime in the first millennium B.C., and that the predominantly Negro peoples who once inhabited the Abyssinian highlands had long before this been pushed southwards by a Hamitic race from either Africa or Asia. Both groups, Hamites and Semites, are Caucasians and exhibit in their Ethiopian descendants the acquiline nose and finely chiseled features typical of Europeans. However, negroid features are still evident in a number of the population, particularly in the shape of the nose and lips and the darkness of skin, attesting to the substantial intermixture with Negro races that once must have occurred. Negroes may be found today in Ethiopia, largely along its southwestern borders. They have always been regarded with contempt by the Ethiopians, who call them "Shankalla," a term of derision. They were formerly hunted down and captured for use as slaves.

In the centuries following the Arabian migrations to Africa successive waves of the Semitized people of the northern highlands moved south. They conquered and absorbed into their own culture the Hamitic tribes they encountered and imposed upon them their own Semitic language. However, enclaves of non-Semitized aborigines remained here and there, bypassed by the conquerors, and these retain up to the present day their ancient Hamitic tongues and pagan religion. Among these are the so-called "Black Jews" of Abyssinia, the Falashas, who live largely in the mountains of Semien, south of Tigre. Although of Hamitic stock, they are not pagan;

eligion is Judaic, and they are said to owe it to contacts with Arabian states of that faith in pre-Moslem or even pre-Christian .... Much further south, in regions that did not constitute a part of the Ethiopian Empire until the end of the nineteenth century, there are still many Hamitic and some Negro tribes which have never been assimilated. Many of these are pagan, others are Moslem, and a few have turned Christian for reasons of political expediency.

To describe all the different races and tribes in Ethiopia would be a difficult, if not impossible, job in the present state of our knowledge concerning them. There are well over a hundred. The dominant race are the Amharas, descendants of the northern Semitized aborigines. Although they constitute a minority of the total population, they have generally been the ruling group in Ethiopia. Their language, Amharic, is the official language of the Empire and their religion, Christianity, the state religion. They inhabit the central plateau region up to a point some fifty miles north of Gondar and as far south as the Blue Nile in the west. Addis Ababa, the capital, is their southernmost extremity. North of the Amhara-populated regions lie the ancient province of Tigre and the former Italian colony of Eritrea, both Tigrinya-speaking areas. These regions have often been at odds with the Amharas to the south and have a long record of revolt and separatism; a serious flare-up in Tigre occurred as recently as 1943.

Galla groups, speaking a multitude of different dialects, inhabit the area immediately southwest, south, and southeast of an imaginary line running along the Blue Nile through Addis Ababa and along the railway to Dire Dawa. Some of these have infiltrated, beginning in the sixteenth century, into regions along the eastern escarpment of the central plateau as far north as Makalle, and there is a small enclave of them fifty miles east of Lake Tana. The Gallas extend all the way south to the Kenya border, and on their eastern limits are neighbors to the Somali tribes of the Ogaden.

The Gurage people, mainly a pastoral class, live about one hundred fifty miles southwest of the capital. To their south and west are found the Sidamo tribes, a non-Galla Hamitic race speaking many different languages. Negro tribes inhabit the western Ethiopian border areas along a strip some fifty to a hundred miles wide from Eritrea in the north to the Rift Valley in the south. In the northeastern deserts live the Danakil, a savage people hostile to strangers and still reluctant to recognize the authority of the central government.

These are the main races and language groups. However, within each broad grouping are many different tribes, each with its own customs and traditions, and speaking, according to one estimate, a total of forty different languages. The Amharas are Christian, but the majority of Gallas and other tribes are pagan or Moslem. It is impossible to state the size of the present-day population, because no national census has ever been taken. All figures are no better than estimates. The Ethiopian government claimed a total of 19,260,000 in 1953, compared with Italian and British estimates of six to seven million made during and just after World War II.[1] The Ethiopian Ministry of Commerce and Industry made a detailed estimate, by provinces, of only ten million people in 1949. The government's present estimate seems clearly too high. In view of the fact that less than 40 per cent of the country's surface area is either arable or pastoral, it would appear most unlikely that the population should exceed twelve or thirteen million, unless the density of population on the highlands is considerably greater than that of Eritrea or of neighboring Kenya.

When we consider the distribution of this total among the major religious or racial groups, the resulting estimates must be even more shadowy than for the population as a whole. Because of this it will serve no purpose to quote those estimates that have been made by various observers, except to state that in virtually all of them the true Ethiopians, i.e., the descendants of Aksum, comprise no more than one-third of the total and are outnumbered by the more recent Gallas. The proportion of Christians is somewhat higher, since a number of the Gallas and other pagan tribes have been converted, but again exact figures cannot be supplied.

The natural diversity of the many peoples who inhabit the Ethiopian plateau and surrounding lowlands has been perpetuated and

[1] The British and Italian estimates exclude Eritrea, which has a present population of a little over one million.

even intensified over the centuries by their isolation from one another. In large part this is the result of difficult topography, which discourages movement from place to place and thus contributes to inbreeding, self-sufficiency, and provincialism. These results have been accentuated by the sparse contacts the Ethiopians have had with foreign civilizations during their long history. Among all except the educated few, superstition and even witchcraft still flourish despite the formal adherence of a good majority of the people to either the Christian or the Moslem faith. Perhaps 95 per cent of all Ethiopians are illiterate. Ethiopian society is still largely a society based on status, in which the Church and the monarchy play a preponderant role. The value judgments of the vast majority of the people are conditioned by ethical, cultural, and social patterns far removed from our own.

To the traveler in the interior Ethiopians are for the most part friendly, with a natural courtesy that has always been proverbial. Some tribes, on the other hand, are dangerous, among them the Danakil, the Issa, the Karayu, and the Ankober. These nomadic or seminomadic tribes are bitter enemies of their neighbors, and occasionally defy the authority of the central government. During 1955, for example, there was a rebellion of the Issa tribe, who inhabit the Dire Dawa area. Their hostility made it unsafe for strangers to wander alone out of town after dark. Government troops attempted to push them away from this populated center by capturing their water wells, and a battle ensued. Other tribes are a menace because murder and mutilation are a part of their social code. The Danakil are notorious in this respect. A member of this tribe who has never killed and mutilated another male is not considered to have sufficiently demonstrated his manhood to become eligible for marriage.

Despite the laudable emphasis of the present government on education, the movement is still too recent, and the facilities available too few, to have had more than a tangential effect on the general cultural level of the population. Ethiopians are still profoundly ignorant of the world around them. Most are born, live, and die in the same small community and are intensely provincial, even tribal, in attachments and loyalties. The veneer of civilization that the country has attained to in its educated class is, with few exceptions, extremely thin. The traveler in the interior sees these people in all their primitive and self-sufficient simplicity, living in grass-thatched mud huts, keeping a few cows or goats, and tilling the soil in the manner of their ancestors for hundreds and even thousands of years. The vast majority are blithely unconcerned about "progress," and are little moved by monetary incentives. They are extremely poor, but not unhappy, in marked contrast to the semisophisticated young people of the capital and one or two other urban centers who have had a taste of the outside world. The political, social, and economic advances described in later chapters of this book have so far made no more than a ripple in the placid daily life of the vast majority of the people.

Ethiopian education is still in its elementary stages. Before the Italian occupation not more than a dozen government schools existed in the whole of Ethiopia. In addition there were some privately run foreign mission schools, plus the centers of lay and religious instruction which the Ethiopian Church had maintained for centuries. A few score students had been sent abroad to study at government expense. Since the restoration a great deal has been done to broaden the educational base, but clearly this is only a beginning and a far cry from the Emperor's announced ideal of compulsory mass education for his people. In 1956 there were approximately 70,000 Ethiopian children attending government schools, with perhaps an equal number receiving private and religious instruction, the whole comprising only a very small fraction—certainly under 5 per cent—of the school-age population.[2] Most of the 500-odd existing schools are elementary, giving instruction up to the eighth grade only. Only a few are secondary; in 1956 the total number of students at secondary schools was less than 2,500. There is also one college, the University College in Addis Ababa, offering a four-year preparatory course leading to professional or university studies abroad. At present, about 11 per cent of the Ethiopian government's budget goes for educational expenditures.

The quality of most of the teaching is inferior, often no more than

[2] There were also some thirteen thousand school children in Eritrea.

a case of the blind leading the blind. Fewer than one-fifth of the teachers are foreign, and some of these are incompetent. Moreover, even the relatively few students who attend and complete secondary school in Ethiopia find it difficult to overcome the paralyzing effect of pressures toward social conformity. They remain too tradition-centered and subservient in their attitude toward their superiors. On the other hand, the little education they have received often engenders a reaction of arrogance toward foreigners. For one reason or another, most Ethiopians who have had a little schooling quickly conclude that they have learned enough.

Foreign teachers in Ethiopia appear to agree that Ethiopian students in general, although willing to learn, are not adept at creative thinking and independent study. They learn their lessons in order to pass, but they seldom truly comprehend what they have absorbed. Textbook answers are returned on examination forms, but there is little constructive criticism of the teacher's views either on paper or in classroom discussion. Even in the University College independent research and original thinking are seldom encountered. The explanation for this passive attitude seems to be the long tradition of imperial rule and the pervasive oppression of individual initiative and thinking still associated with it, which surrounds the Ethiopian from birth, and which cannot be overcome in the relatively brief period of classroom exposure. Rank and status have for long been of central importance in the Ethiopian's approach to society. The delegation of authority has traditionally been regarded as a lowering of the status of superiors and an unwarranted elevation of subordinates. This feeling is apparently still very widespread and may account for the persistent unwillingness, to be found in almost all Ethiopians except those who have spent many years abroad, to assume responsibility on their own. These deep-seated attitudes, which cannot be laid aside voluntarily, are probably the single most inhibiting influence in Ethiopian education today.

In Ethiopia, as in many another underdeveloped country, the institution of land tenure is the key to an understanding of numerous problems, because it is the point of convergence of political, economic, and social forces. Until very recently, the institutions surrounding the ownership and use of land were distinctly medieval, if not feudal, in character, and although certain legal reforms have lately been attempted to abolish or at least mitigate some of the inequities under the system, the problem is far from solved. Cases involving disputes over land are the main occupation of the courts in a country where title deeds are rare, where exact measurement of land was until very recently unknown (and is still not widely practiced), and where the notion of private individual holdings is just beginning to find acceptance. No adequate study has ever been made of Ethiopian land tenure, one of the reasons being that it is extremely complex and information concerning it is difficult to come by.

There is no doubt, however, that the institution has always been central in the life of the people, and that their destinies have been ruled by it even more than by the Church. Closely bound up with it was a notorious system of serfdom known as the *gabar* system. (The institution of slavery will be mentioned separately later; it was not in theory directly concerned with land tenure.) The term *gabar* applies to a peasant tenant from whom a landlord has the right to demand certain services and wealth in return for the use of his land. In theory this right attached to the land and not to the tenant. In practice, however, since personal mobility was circumscribed by, among other things, the universality of the system, the *gabar* was virtually a serf, if not a slave. Although *gabars* had the right of appeal to the Emperor, few of them were able or willing to make the long journey to the capital.

Most Ethiopians, apart from the relatively few landowners, were *gabars*. They owed a variety of dues, formerly payable in kind, as taxes to the central government, and in addition paid rent in the form of tribute or services to the landowners. Frequently the landowner was the government itself, in the person of *rases, dedjazmatches,* or other officials combining high military rank with civil duties, or simply soldiers who had served the Emperor well and who had been rewarded with a grant of land. These officials were not granted absolute title to the land itself, but authorized to collect from the *gabars* the taxes due to the government. *Gabars* working on lands belonging to the Church, which was tax-exempt, were required to furnish their labor for miscellaneous services, as well as a part (usually one-third) of the produce as rent. Individual land ownership was rare. Over large parts of the northern provinces, and in Eritrea, land could be owned in common by a whole family or clan or community. In theory, and this was vigorously asserted by certain emperors from time to time, all the land in the country belonged to the Emperor.

Today a large part of the land is held royally, another large part is held by the Church, with much of the remainder in the hands of various powerful absentee landlords. Exactly what the distinction is between lands held by the State as such and by the imperial family is not clear. The point is of recent origin and had no importance in the days when the Emperor and the State were synonymous. Vast areas of land were conquered by the Emperor Menelik II during his far-ranging campaigns in the south at the end of the last century. Many of these were added outright to his personal domain; some were granted to his favorites and loyal soldiery; a few were left in the hands of the conquered peoples. The amount of land owned by the individual freeholders actually working it is small, but perhaps increasing. No precise figure can be given on its extent; a fair guess would be no more than 10 per cent of the total.

The system of land tenure is further complicated by the fact that much of the land throughout the country is burdened with special status and hereditary rights. *Rest* tenure applies to land to which hereditary ownership attaches. *Gult* tenure signifies land on which the Emperor has granted away some or all of his rights to tribute. Variations and combinations of these forms of tenure are numerous and are interwoven with the varying structure of imperial, Church, and private ownership to form a pattern of incredible complexity.

The power of the *gabar* system lay in the manner in which payment of the various taxes and tributes was made, that is, in kind. The system of payment opened the way for all kinds of extortion. After the imperial restoration in 1941, a reformed provincial administrative system based on salaried offices was set up, and the system was seriously weakened. The most serious abuses were eliminated by the postwar changeover to a fiscal system in which taxes are payable in cash instead of in kind. In addition, many of the petty taxes, services, and fees previously levied on the peasants were consolidated into a single fixed tax and tithe upon all land. The government has proclaimed its intention of eliminating the *gabar* system altogether, but this has not yet been done directly by any specific law. One eminent authority on Ethiopia writes, and this remains true, that "It is difficult to say what is the actual position in Ethiopia today with regard to the payment of rent by the old tribute and services. The greatly increased use of currency must have affected the position even apart from any regulations."[3]

The complex system of land tenure, and the *gabar* system with which it was formerly intimately associated, are principal elements in the structure of Ethiopian tribal society. Another element, until very recently also of great importance, was the institution of slavery. Some observers of long residence in Ethiopia maintain that this still exists, although much modified, despite the strenuous efforts of the Ethiopian government to stamp it out. It is known, for example, that two runaway slaves sought protection from the British authorities as late as 1944, and the British Council of Civil Liberties in 1947 claimed that there were some two million slaves still in the country. This estimate must be seriously questioned, since it is difficult to understand on what basis it could possibly have been made. Ethiopians generally maintain that the institution is dead, although they admit that some former slaves may still be voluntarily attached to their masters. This result is quite consistent with the most recent law on the subject, that of 1942, which abolished the legal basis of slavery.[4] Under it slaves who were ill-treated, or who for other reasons decided to leave their masters, were free to do so, and presumably most have by now taken advantage of this freedom. Many others must have elected to stay with their former masters for personal or economic reasons, but this could hardly be called slavery.

The institution has thus just about disappeared, and can properly

[3] Margery Perham, *The Government of Ethiopia* (London, 1946), p. 235.

[4] A Proclamation to Provide for the Abolition of the Legal Basis of Slavery and Certain Other Matters, No. 22 of 1942, *Negarit Gazeta*, August 26, 1942.

be considered of historical interest only. The interested reader will find an excellent short survey of Ethiopian slavery in Perham.[5]

Another formerly important social and political institution among the Galla tribes is the so-called *gada* system. It continues to exist in greatly modified form. Curiously, very little information is available about this from educated Ethiopians of the younger generation, most of whom profess a complete ignorance of the term. In the old Galla society, before its inundation by the centralized administrative system of the Amharas, the term *gada* referred to a system of age grades, whereby the entire organization of tribal life was divided into stages of eight years' duration. Each tribe was divided into about ten groups, called *gadas,* the particular *gada* to which a member of the tribe belonged being determined solely by his age. The penultimate *gada* comprised the ruling group, which inherited power from the outgoing group of elders. The system was highly democratic, in contrast to the monarchical and hierarchical system of the Amharas. It has been considerably changed and weakened, however, by the imposition of Amhara rule, and also by the adoption of Islam by great numbers of Gallas. Its significance today is purely local and partly historical.

If there is one element whose preeminence in the social structure of Ethiopia, today as formerly, is beyond dispute, it is the Ethiopian Orthodox Church. Although its adherents comprise a minority of the population, outnumbered by the followers of Islam and by the pagan tribes, it is intertwined with the political forces of the country in a way that greatly enhances its strength. Christianity has been the official religion of the Ethiopian State since the fourth century A.D. The revised Ethiopian constitution of 1955, by specifically stating that "The Emperor shall always profess the Ethiopian Orthodox faith" (Article 126), rules out the possibility of a Moslem Emperor or one of any other faith. The Emperor has always been the secular head of the Ethiopian Church, as well as head of the State. The same article referred to states that "The name of the Emperor shall be mentioned in all religious services," thus emphasizing anew the close connection between Church and State that has always existed in Ethiopia.

[5] Perham, *The Government of Ethiopia*, chap. 12.

Religion has always played an important role in the daily lives of primitive peoples, and this is very definitely still the case in Ethiopia. The younger generation of the towns, especially those who have had a degree of schooling, sometimes profess a spirit of agnosticism, perhaps more from a desire to be "modern" than from inner conviction. Whatever its basis, this agnostic spirit seems to be growing and is serving to reinforce the long-standing antagonism of the Ethiopian Church to social progress. Some of its leaders today recognize that change is unavoidable, that the old religious attitudes are incompatible with rapid economic development. But the extreme conservatism, even backwardness, of the Ethiopian Church as a whole, and the central position it still occupies among the people, are good evidence that the tempo of political and economic advance is bound to remain slow for a long time to come.

Let us take a closer look at this extremely important Ethiopian institution, the Ethiopian Orthodox Church, and see what it represents and how it is bound up with other social and political elements.

The Ethiopian Orthodox Church has from its earliest days been associated with the Egyptian Coptic Church of Alexandria. This relationship dates, as noted previously, from the consecration of Frumentius, the founder of Christianity in Ethiopia, by the Patriarch of Alexandria in the fourth century A.D. It has been perpetuated up to the present day. Until 1948, when a concordat was signed with the Alexandrine Church, permitting a native Ethiopian to become Archbishop, the Church of Egypt had always appointed one of its own members to this position. This appointee was a foreigner to Ethiopia, not only in nationality, but usually in every other respect as well. The typical Archbishop knew nothing of the country or its inhabitants, felt his mission there to be tantamount to exile, and could not speak to priests and people or offer prayers in their language. For these reasons the Ethiopian Church long sought to obtain full autonomy in Church matters and to appoint an Archbishop from among its own clergy. These rights were at last recognized by the mother church a decade ago, thus ending eight centuries of effort on the part of the Ethiopian Church to achieve independence.

The Ethiopian Church is monophysite in character, meaning that

—in contrast to most other branches of Christianity—it holds Christ's nature to be single and not dual, his manhood being absorbed in his divinity. This subtle theological difference was one that caused much dispute and ill-feeling between Jesuits and Abyssinians when it first came to light some centuries ago. Ethiopian Christianity also differs from western forms in certain other respects, mostly minor, as in religious observances and ritual (certain pagan rites have been retained in church services), and in the composition of the Bible.

Fast days and holy days are extremely numerous in Ethiopia, and there are a vast number of priests and churches in the country. Some have described the country as "priest-ridden"; estimates of the number of priests run as high as 20 per cent of the male population. The church is the center of village life. Although the villagers may reside in pest-infested, ramshackle, one-room huts, the church is certain to be large, well-built, and relatively clean. Despite the formal adherence of a large majority of the people to religion, sorcery and witchcraft are powerfully respected and widely engaged in, sometimes even by the priests of the Church in an unofficial capacity. The clergy, owing to their position of authority, are generally opposed to change; many priests are ignorant and lazy, and few are above exploiting for their own profit the simple religious faith of the people. Every Ethiopian Christian has a "soul-confessor," who extracts a heavy fee for the remission of sin. The priests mostly live in idleness on the labor of their *gabars*. In 1933, the Emperor publicly condemned their fighting and drunkenness and cupidity during the *tazkar,* or memorial to the dead.[6]

Of course, not all the clergy are of this low caliber. The *debteroch* —cantors and lay scholars—have been almost the only class in the country until recent times which could read and write and had the rudiments of an education. The Church maintained centers of religious and lay instruction for hundreds of years before the first Ethiopian state school was established by Menelik II in 1905. Today it is claimed that as many Ethiopian children attend the Church

[6] *Courrier d'Ethiopie*, May 12, 1933, cited in Perham, *The Government of Ethiopia*, p. 113.

schools as attend the public schools (some 70,000 in each), but the level of instruction in Church schools is even lower than in public schools, and the curriculum is very limited. In recent years a theological seminary has been established in Addis Ababa for the education of those desiring to enter the priesthood.

In political matters, Church influence is still immensely powerful, though probably on the wane. The Emperor has found it expedient to move very circumspectly even in secular matters; in religious affairs he is doubly careful to observe all the forms of Church authority and to avoid any action that might give the clergy the impression that they are gradually being edged out of the picture. Nevertheless, this is what is happening as democratic institutions slowly evolve in Ethiopia and as political functions increase in scope and complexity. The Church will find in time, as it long ago found in Europe, that it must yield power in secular matters. This may be all to the good, in so far as it forces the Church itself to clean house and rid itself of corruption and ignorance.

To complete this brief cultural commentary a word should be said about the importance of Islam in Ethiopia, the state of the arts and sciences, and the sociological characteristics of Ethiopians in general.

Although Ethiopia's Moslems constitute some one-third of the country's population, their influence on the contemporary Ethiopian scene is completely overshadowed by the dominating political position of Amhara Christianity. As we have seen, Moslem armies in past centuries often threatened to, and on occasion did, overrun the whole of Ethiopia. It is likely the country would be Moslem today had not the Portuguese intervened in 1541. The demented Lidj Yasu, successor to Menelik II, embraced this religion and would have made it the State religion, had it not been for the united opposition of the Shoan nobility and the foreign legations. As late as 1935-40 the Italians, desiring to undermine the authority of the Ethiopian Orthodox Church, pursued a policy of deliberately favoring Islam in Ethiopia. Today, however, Islam is not a force politically. Each year at the great feast of Ramadan signaling the end of the longest period of Moslem fasting, the leaders of the Moslem community in Ethiopia present themselves at the imperial palace to convey expressions of good will and loyalty to their Christian Emperor. Yet it is significant that the Amharas are still so distrustful of Islam that very few Moslems are to be found in high positions in the Ethiopian government.

Native Ethiopian contributions to the realm of the arts and sciences are conspicuous by their absence. There exists a body of Church literature, some of it ancient, but it is mostly concerned with hagiography or the laudation of kings. There is a stereotyped form of picture painting which apparently has not changed through the centuries; the same styles can be found in old manuscripts and in canvases hawked by street urchins in Addis Ababa today. Architecture is nonexistent, as is sculpture. There is a form of music, played on crude and simple instruments, but to American ears, at least, it is unimaginative, monotonous, strident, and primitive. Only in the last few years, among the younger generation, has there been some stirring of creative talent, resulting in the writing of some books and poems and in the production of some art. There have always been some native handicrafts, such as pottery and basket making, as well as weaving. Of science there is as yet no inkling. The first Ethiopian physician has recently completed his studies abroad and is now employed at one of the hospitals in the capital. To the author's knowledge, there is still not a single fully qualified Ethiopian civil engineer. The Ethiopian people have shown themselves to be remarkably uncreative; they were not even acquainted with the wheel until it was introduced from Europe. With very few exceptions, among them the stone churches of Lalibela and the castles of Fasilidas at Gondar, they have contributed absolutely nothing to the culture of the world. And even these few achievements, as we have seen, are disputed by many as probably foreign in execution if not in design.

Contemporary observers, as well as travelers who visited Ethiopia in earlier times, seem fairly well agreed on the main characteristics of the Ethiopian people. Probably the most marked of these is self-satisfaction. A former English consul to Ethiopia during Theodore's reign, Walter Plowden, wrote of them in his *Travels in Abyssinia*: "Once vanquish the idea that they are perfect, that they are the favoured people of the earth, that nothing can be taught them, and they will be quick and intelligent to learn and to imitate." The same observer lists also among their defects indolence, "overweening vanity, entire ignorance of the world beyond Abyssinia," and "aversion to the smallest change." "They have a great contempt for other nations and scarcely know, or do not care, if any exist or not."[7] On the other hand, he mentions their pleasing manners, their humor, their generosity, and their practical philosophy that leads them to prefer laughter to tears. The Ethiopians are undoubtedly courageous in war, as they demonstrated in Korea, and they are easygoing and generally indulgent. They are often cruel to animals, perhaps more from ignorance and from lack of forethought than from malice, but in general kind and hospitable to strangers. They are unimaginative and uninventive, and stubbornly conservative, as remarked by more than one writer. Tellez, a Jesuit writer of the early eighteenth century, remarks that their reply to a criticism of one of their institutions was: "This same is and ever was the Form of Government in [their] Country, and it will cause great Troubles to alter it."[8] Ethiopians are generally lax in their sexual life, with divorce extremely frequent and easy for those not married by the Church. In former times even the imperial house was known for its widespread practice of concubinage.

To what extent the negative side of the Ethiopian's character may be due to the environmental conditions under which he is born and raised, and to what extent to inherent intellectual shortcomings, is difficult to say. It is popular nowadays to assert that all peoples are basically alike in intelligence, but the point cannot be proved because of the impossibility of isolating the environmental factor. The biologist Julian Huxley observes that "the existence of marked genetic differences in physical characters (as between yellow, black, white, and brown) makes it *prima facie* likely that differences in intelligence and temperament exist also."[9] Whatever the facts of the matter may be, the Ethiopian requires almost constant supervision and correction, even in the simplest jobs, and will not readily adopt even the most obvious improvements. Thus, for example, one daily sees the women

[7] *Travels in Abyssinia* (1868), pp. 396, 395, 131.

[8] B. Tellez, *Travels of the Jesuits in Ethiopia* (1710), p. 54.

[9] "Eugenics and Society," *Man Stands Alone* (New York, 1941).

in Addis Ababa and elsewhere trudging miles with a heavy water jug or bundle of sticks on their backs, but never using a hand-drawn cart. Such a vehicle could be easily and cheaply fashioned if a man put his mind to it, and it is certainly beyond neither the means nor the ability of Ethiopians to construct. It would eliminate a lot of back-breaking work. But although the transportation of the heaviest loads by motor truck is a familiar sight to all living near a road or in the towns, the example seems lost on the ordinary Ethiopian. Even horse-drawn or other animal-powered carts are rarely used, despite the great numbers of animals which are available for this work.[10]

The average Ethiopian is perfectly content with his lot and sees little reason to change his ways. Change, however, is in the nature of things and will be forced on him, willing or not, as his country develops. The process will not be painless, and the measure of his adjustment to it will be found in his cooperation with, or resistance to, the march of progress.

[10] In the capital and one or two other towns a two-wheeled horse-drawn open carriage known as a "gharry" is employed for passenger transportation. This was introduced during the Italian occupation.

IV

Government Structure and Administration

The most important fact to be kept in mind about the government of Ethiopia is that it is an absolute monarchy and in no sense democratic.[1] The Emperor is the supreme authority, despite the existence of a written constitution, and appoints all subordinates. He takes a personal hand in nearly all affairs of state and, indeed, in former times he literally was the State. Under the growing complexity of modern government he has been obliged to let others share with him certain responsibilities and duties, and has delegated authority to ministers and other subordinates. This development has been virtually forced on him by the physical incompatibility of one-man rule with the functioning of a modern state, and has been accepted only gradually and with extreme reluctance. The reason lies in the traditional viewpoint that delegation of authority is unseemly in the eyes of both superior and subordinate. Thus it is that even today the Emperor must be consulted in relatively minor matters of administration which in more advanced countries are decided routinely by a host of lower officials. Even on the ministerial level the assumption of individual authority and responsibility in matters of any moment is a rarity, and it is still all too frequently the experience of foreigners to

[1] Reference is to the federal government; the local structure of government in Eritrea is, at least in theory, democratic.

discover, when they call upon a minister, that he has gone to the *ghibbi* (palace) to wait upon the Emperor. Not only ministers but officials of all ranks, whether they want to obtain a specific favor or merely to forward their careers, call regularly at the palace to be seen by and to bow to the Emperor. This ceremony, known in Amharic as *dedj tenat,* is a weekly occurrence. The rigidity and ponderousness it introduces into the machinery of government is one reason for the inefficiency and interminable delays of Ethiopian administration.

Despite some paper reforms the Ethiopian government is still very much influenced by the power of status and tradition. This is an elusive, though very real, factor in Ethiopian history. Titles are revered in Ethiopia, regardless of whether their holders are competent to exercise their official duties or not. Machiavelli's observation that "titles do not reflect honor on men, but rather men on their titles" does not seem to be generally understood in Ethiopia. Hence the apparent necessity of placating so many of the reactionary old guard by appointing them to high office, and hence the feeling among foreign observers that the government is dragging its feet. The traditions of centuries are not easily set aside, and it will probably not be until the older generation has expired and the rising group of foreign-educated Ethiopians has completely filled the administrative ranks that a really widespread and basic reform can be carried out.

Despite the people's reverence for titles, they have seldom been hereditary in Ethiopia, and a feudal nobility in the sense of a proper-tied and titled class with hereditary rights as in Europe never arose. Neither did the Church, powerful as it was, ever presume to overrule the Emperor or to delimit its own rights and privileges. These varied, as did those of the nobility, with the weakness or strength of their protagonists vis-à-vis the Emperor, who himself, as we have seen in Chapter II, was at times Emperor in name only.

Nevertheless, in theory the Emperor has always been supreme. In this supremacy he has been supported by the Solomonian legend, which effectively established the imperial family as heirs of the biblical promises to David. Usurpers of the throne, when they appeared, were considerably weakened in their position by their inability to claim this sacred connection for themselves. The Emperor Haile

Selassie I has sought to fortify his position by repeating the claim of Solomonian ancestry in the constitution. The legendary nature of this claim seems clear; moreover, in view of the extreme laxity of marriage in Ethiopia, and the widespread practice of concubinage even in the imperial house from ancient times, it would seem that no dynastic claim could be made with any certainty; all this apart from the fact that the earliest kings of Ethiopia of which we have any knowledge, those of ancient Aksum, openly professed to be pagans. Nevertheless, the legend has great force and still exerts immense influence among Ethiopians, who appear to derive a psychological lift from the pretense that they are the chosen people.

The supreme authority of the Emperor, who until recently, as has been indicated, suffered no limitations on his power except those he was obliged to recognize by force of arms, has under Haile Selassie I undergone the beginnings of a remarkable evolution, initiated by the Emperor himself as the result of his voluntary recognition of certain popular rights as expressed in the constitution of 1931. Perhaps in the fullness of time some such limitation of the imperial power would have developed in any case, as it has elsewhere. But Haile Selassie chose to hasten the process in a manner unprecedented in the history of the country. The constitution of 1931 defined the power and prerogatives of the Emperor, provided for the succession to the throne, recognized certain civil rights and duties, set up a puppet legislature, confirmed the ministers in their duties, provided for an annual budget, and established a regular judiciary. However, it remained for the most part a dead letter.

It was succeeded in 1955 by a revised and expanded document. The new constitution, promulgated by the Emperor on the twenty-fifth anniversary of his coronation, went considerably beyond its predecessor both in scope and in detail. (Some of its provisions regarding the relationship of the Ethiopian Orthodox Church to the imperial power have already been cited.) It is possible to go into the 1955 constitution in detail, examining carefully each of its provisions and comparing them with those of its predecessor, but it is doubtful whether the true importance and significance of the document can be assessed in this manner. As the Emperor himself stated in his throne speech to Parliament of November 4, 1955, "No single document, however profound and comprehensive, can, of itself, bring about far-reaching and fundamental constitutional progress. No constitutional progress can take effect unless it is rooted in the fundamental traditions, customs, habits, and predilections, as well as the legal customs, of the society upon which it is based." The Emperor was clearly aware of the difficult problems involved in making this new constitution a living document.

If the 1955 constitution is not to remain a dead letter like its predecessor, it will have to be accompanied by a veritable revolution of thought and action on the part of both its administrators and its beneficiaries. For it can by no stretch of the imagination be maintained that this semidemocratic, semimonarchical document is "rooted in the fundamental traditions" of Ethiopian society. It is, if anything, so foreign to those traditions in some respects as to be scarcely recognizable as deriving from them. Educated Ethiopians, as well as foreigners, regard the new constitution as too advanced to be practical for some years to come. At all events, its meaning seems to be lost on the vast majority of Ethiopians, if, indeed, they so much as know of its existence.

No doubt the Emperor is aware that it will not be possible to realize immediately the principle of parliamentary rule, independence of the judiciary, or the numerous rights of free speech, press, and assembly guaranteed by the constitution to the people. But by example and precept, and by preparing the institutional basis for progress, he probably hopes to facilitate and to guide the political development of his country in a chosen direction. The promulgation of the new constitution on the occasion of the Emperor's Silver Jubilee Coronation was probably calculated to impress foreign observers of the Ethiopian scene and to enhance the prestige of the Ethiopian government abroad. Its timing may also have been influenced by the fact that a liberal and democratic constitution for Eritrea had been drawn up by the United Nations some three years before.

The new constitution provides for an enlargement of Parliament and for the direct election of one of its houses, the Chamber of Deputies, by secret ballot of qualified voters. The other house, the Senate, is appointed by the Emperor. An electoral law has been prepared and was apparently the basis for the elections to Parliament in September 1957. Under it qualified men and women over twenty-one reportedly voted for deputies to represent them in the national legislature. A considerable to-do was made over the results, with the Emperor personally addressing the successful candidates to impress upon them their rights and duties under the new constitution.

To what extent democratic procedures have actually been invoked in the elections is another matter. It is difficult to see how the popular election of deputies as provided for in the constitution could actually have been carried out, since vital and census statistics are practically nonexistent, maps are unavailable, and the mass of the electorate is profoundly ignorant of both the purposes and the procedures of voting. The government's claim that two million Ethiopians voted in the 1957 elections has been called "entirely unbelievable" by one observer, who adds that "even in Addis Ababa many well-schooled people did not know that an election was going on."

Only a small percentage of the population is literate; most Ethiopians have no conception whatsoever of politics. There are, in fact, no political parties or shades of political opinion, and there is no evidence to suggest that parties or opinions are developing under the greater freedoms guaranteed by the new constitution. On what basis, then, did the voters choose? They presumably voted as they were directed to vote by the elders of their tribes. No other conclusion is reasonable. Direct popular elections, in the fullest sense of the term, are still a long way off.

Article 86 of the new constitution deals with the actual legislative power of Parliament. It is so brief as to permit of full quotation here:

"Laws may be proposed to either or both Chambers of Parliament: (a) by the Emperor, or (b) by ten or more members of either Chamber of Parliament, except that every proposal involving an increase in governmental expenditure or a new or increased tax shall first be presented to the Chamber of Deputies."

Thus the lawmaking initiative of Parliament is confined to a group initiative. Individual members may not propose legislation. This may serve to restrict the actual volume of legislation, since the old saw that a committee is a group of men who individually can do nothing and who collectively decide that nothing can be done applies with special force to Ethiopia. The committee system has become a favorite stratagem there for the shifting of responsibility. On the other hand, the individual members of Parliament may well find strength in numbers and protection in the impersonality of the group.

However this may be, Article 86 contains all that the constitution has to say about Parliament's legislative power. Article 88 states that the proposed legislation will become law if approved by the Emperor. If not, it is dead, and cannot be passed over the Emperor's veto.

It should be noted that the Emperor himself can propose legislation, either personally or through his ministers; that "in cases of emergency that arise when the Chambers are not sitting" the Emperor may issue decrees having the force of law, which cease to be law only if later revoked by Parliament (Article 92); that the Emperor has the right to dissolve Parliament without stated cause; that he has the right to appoint ministers and mayors, to declare war or a national emergency, to exercise supreme control over foreign affairs, to ratify treaties, to coin, print, and issue money, and to "take all measures that may be necessary to ensure . . . the defense and integrity of the Empire [or] the safety and welfare of its inhabitants" (Article 36). He exercises "the supreme authority over all the affairs of the Empire" (Article 26).

The Emperor's powers, as can be seen, are thus extremely broad, even on paper. Moreover, the thing to remember about the Ethiopian government, above all, is that it is a government of men and not of laws. Status and tradition, however they may be circumscribed by constitutional arrangements, remain and will long remain the real and final arbiter in all things. Ethiopians will not allow themselves to be dominated by legalistics, and the Emperor is not likely to allow a constitutional phrase to put limitations on his real power. Humpty-Dumpty's discourse with Alice illustrates the point: " 'When I use a word,' Humpty-Dumpty said, in a rather scornful tone, 'it means just what I choose it to mean—neither more nor less.' 'The question is,' said Alice, 'whether you *can* make words mean so many different things.' 'The question is,' said Humpty-Dumpty, 'which is to be master—that's all.' "

The Parliament formed under the constitution of 1931 played no more than a decorative role on the Ethiopian scene. Laws were drawn up, not by its members, but by ministers and their foreign advisers, and Parliament rubber-stamped them. Its meetings were closed to the public (though the new constitution envisages open sessions), and news of its doings seldom appeared in the press. No news of elections of deputies or appointments of senators was ever, to the author's knowledge, made public. Parliament was only heard from when the press reported the Emperor's addresses to it (usually delivered at its annual opening). These addresses were never an outline of needs and proposals accompanied by an exhortation for legislative action, as in the United States, for example; they were instead confined entirely to a review of past events. There was no need for the Emperor to explain and exhort: no Ethiopian parliamentarian ever had the temerity to reject the Emperor's proposals in favor of his own. The new constitution requires members of Parliament to take an oath of loyalty to the Emperor and to swear that they will obey the constitution and perform their duties "conscientiously and without fear or favor." It remains to be seen whether, in fact, such a spirit of independence, initiative, and responsibility can be developed.

The judicial system as it exists today is largely a postwar product. Starting from the top, there is a Supreme Imperial Court (the only court specifically mentioned in the new constitution), a High Court, provincial courts, and regional and communal courts. These courts were established and their functions defined by the Administration of Justice Proclamation of 1942. The jurisdiction of these various courts is defined by law; any litigant or defendant may, on appeal, have his case transferred to the High Court, which at times goes on circuit. Appeal is from a lower to the next higher court and is usually final. The Supreme Imperial Court hears appeals from the High Court, and is of appellate jurisdiction only. It is presided over by the Afa Negus (Mouth of the Emperor), who sits with two High Court judges designated in each case by the presiding judge of the High

Court. Since the restoration of 1941, the presiding judge of the High Court has always been a foreigner.

Special courts, called Kadis and Naibas Councils, have been set up to deal with questions concerning the personal status of Moslems (marriage, inheritance, and the like). Such courts apply Moslem law only. Foreigners, formerly accorded special treatment, now come under the full jurisdiction of Ethiopian law.

Almost all the laws in the country are of recent origin, most of them enacted since the restoration in 1941. An ancient book of laws called the *Fetha Negast* is probably the oldest collection of written law in Ethiopia. A thirteenth-century compilation of ecclesiastical, Roman, and Moslem law introduced into Ethiopia in the seventeenth century, it long served as the basic reference for the settlement of disputes in that country. It is still honored and cited in Ethiopian courts, but it has largely fallen into disuse outside of the ecclesiastical domain. Ethiopia's first modern written laws were issued in the form of decrees during the regency of Haile Selassie I. They were sometimes printed for distribution, sometimes merely posted in a prominent place in the capital. It was only after the restoration of the Ethiopian government in 1941 that the practice of printing all laws in an official journal, the *Negarit Gazeta,* was introduced. Certain abuses remain to be ironed out—some regulations having the force of law have never appeared in this publication, and many laws have not appeared in print until long after their promulgation—but the *Gazeta* is nonetheless a great step forward.

Ethiopian law is still largely customary, despite the considerable volume of postwar legislation. There is very little in the way of real law, or law codes, in the Western manner; the most that can be said is that there are numerous miscellaneous regulations alongside a vast amount of customary law. In civil law there exists a company law that is very brief and inadequate. There are also some fiscal laws and a penal code which has lately been revised. This is the total of substantive law. There are no effective codes of procedure. A European commission has been working for years on a codification of civil, criminal, and commercial law—much of it newly created—and on codes of civil and criminal procedure. As already indicated, most litigation is in land disputes, but there are also a great number of criminal cases. Almost every infraction of law is regarded as criminal, and the distinction between criminal and civil is badly blurred.

Most Ethiopian judges have no legal qualifications. The grayer the head, the more respect it is accorded. Bribery and corruption are common, and since the law is rarely precise, a defendant has no assurance of impartial justice. Precedents have no force and are seldom applied, so that similar cases may be decided quite differently before different judges.

Public hanging is sometimes still carried out in the capital, although each execution must receive the previous confirmation of the Emperor. Flogging is also practiced. In former times it was customary to cut off the hand of a thief, or the right arm and left leg of a deserter in war. The revised constitution, however, now specifically forbids "cruel and inhuman punishment" (Article 57).

There is no question of the courts in Ethiopia passing on the constitutionality of any law, i.e., of serving as an independent arbiter between the people, on the one hand, and the executive and legislative power on the other.

Trial by jury is not practiced. Sometimes trial itself is dispensed with altogether; many a vagrancy suspect has simply been spirited off to work in the gold mines at Adola. In 1955 houseboys in Addis Ababa were required by the police to obtain written statements from their employers, lest being found without such evidence of employment they be dispatched to Adola. It is a not uncommon sight to see several policemen carrying rifles herding a group of ragged children through the streets.

When a case goes to trial it may take years before a judgment is reached, especially in land disputes. The time-consuming nature of court action is such that businessmen in Ethiopia will often submit to what they regard as patent injustices, e.g., the arbitrary imposition of taxes, rather than waste time contesting such abuses in court. Moreover, the courts' decisions are often bizarre by Western standards. In a 1955 case involving a foreign importer who had brought suit against a buyer for failure to pay for Eth.$5,000 of goods received, the decision of the court, after lengthy delay, was that the defendant must pay off the debt at the rate of Eth.$20 a month. The money was to be collected through the court. After calling at the court several times to find, in the first instance, that the defendant had not yet deposited the funds, and in the second, that the court officials were absent, the company decided to write off the loss. Such cases have been all too frequent in Ethiopia, as any businessman in the country will confirm.

If the Emperor or a high government official presses a case against someone, the defendant has little hope of securing an impartial decision, the new constitution to the contrary notwithstanding.[2] Often the judges do not even know what the law is, or if there is one concerning the matter at hand. Whether or not a law is adhered to seems to be a matter of its convenience or inconvenience; it is all too likely to be disregarded where sufficient pressure is brought to bear from on high. The ordinary Ethiopian is cowed by the courts, and will accept their decision without murmur. He has been brought up to respect and obey authority.

Further, there is a tendency in Ethiopia to assume that where a law exists the offense does not occur. Many laws are enacted and later left unenforced, or are unenforceable because no provision is made for their implementation. The law of 1950 prohibiting urinating or defecating in public, for example, is neither enforced nor enforceable because the government never got around to the construction of the necessary public latrines, and there are practically none in Ethiopian houses. Thoroughness is not one of the Ethiopian virtues.

Arbitrariness and highhandedness are common in the administration of the law by petty officials, mostly uneducated men with a typical bureaucratic disdain for the long-suffering public. Their rulings are particularly hard on the common people, most of whom would not dream of contesting an administrative decision by an appeal to higher authority. Those who do, often newcomers to the country, soon realize the futility of the procedure and drop their complaint. Reme-

---

[2] Article 62, for example, provides that any resident of the Empire may bring suit against the government, and Article 110 that judges shall be independent and shall act only in accordance with the law.

dial action through the courts is seldom practicable for reasons already stated.

The assessment of taxes, in particular, is extremely arbitrary. Aside from relatively minor license fees, which are levied by the municipality but are sometimes altered retroactively after correct and full payment has been certified, the businessman's biggest headache is the income tax. There is a law governing this,[3] but it permits of such arbitrary interpretation by the tax authorities that most merchants are unable to tell from year to year where they stand under it. It seems that the categories in which businesses are placed by the Minister of Finance, who alone fixes the tax to be paid, are frequently changed; furthermore, many businesses are arbitrarily classed as "special," and may be liable to a tax of up to 15 per cent of their net income plus 10 per cent surtax on net profit in excess of Eth.$100,000 per year. If no books are kept by the business concerned, as is the case among some of the smaller merchants, a sky-high assessment usually follows. Merchants rarely appeal a high assessment if the amount involved is not greatly excessive, because they lose too much time being kept waiting for a decision by the appeals commission.[4]

The guarantee of civil rights under the new constitution is largely a sop to educated, and in particular foreign, opinion. No Ethiopian in his right mind would dare to mount a soapbox in the middle of the Piazza in Addis Ababa and call for the resignation of a public official on any grounds. No Ethiopian, however educated, would dare to write a letter to a newspaper criticizing a government official, or even government policy, and no newspaper would print such a letter if it received one. It is not a case of brutal oppression by the police of potentially dangerous political elements (although the few threats of

[3] A Proclamation to Provide for the Payment of a Tax by All Individuals and Businesses, No. 107 of 1949, *Negarit Gazeta*, August 27, 1949.

[4] The "waiting treatment" is a favorite Ethiopian stratagem. Aggrieved persons may be told to appear at such and such a time and place for consideration of their complaint. After waiting several hours they may be told that the Ethiopian official has gone out or has not yet arrived, or be told for other reasons to come another day. This can be repeated as often as necessary.

this sort that have arisen have been summarily dealt with). It is simply a case of there not existing, as yet, a sufficiently developed public opinion to take any real interest in the exercise of civil rights, an exercise utterly foreign to the tradition and history of the people. For such delicacies a taste must first be developed. Such a taste is, perhaps, slowly emerging among the educated groups, but most of them are still inhibited by the traditions of the past, as well as by an awareness of the manner in which excessive boldness would be likely to be received. Among Ethiopians forthrightness and directness of speech are shunned, even when the topic is nonpolitical. Although constitutional progress has been notable, Ethiopia is not to be confused with Utopia.[5]

The Emperor Menelik II, who reigned from 1889 to 1913, was apparently the first Ethiopian monarch to introduce the idea of an advisory council and of ministers to aid him in affairs of state. Both institutions suffered various vicissitudes and did not finally and permanently come into being until the reign of Haile Selassie I. The constitution of 1931 makes no mention of any council, but it refers to ministers and specifically to their obligation to deliberate together whenever the Emperor requires an opinion of them on an important matter. After the restoration in 1941 a Council of Ministers was set up, which meets frequently under the chairmanship of the Prime Minister or the Emperor himself to advise on matters of state. A Crown Council also exists, whose membership appears to be rather loose-knit, and whose function is policymaking on the highest level. It consists of the Archbishop, the President of the Senate, and such

---

[5] Such confusion, apparently, has for long existed in the mind of one E. Sylvia Pankhurst, former suffragette and indefatigable champion of the Ethiopian cause. Through the medium of a weekly news sheet and various other publications, this ardent lady has for over twenty years disseminated misinformation about Ethiopia, together with a certain amount of vituperation against those who do not altogether share her enthusiasm. The reader should be aware that Miss Pankhurst has been under subsidy from the Ethiopian government.

princes, ministers, and dignitaries as may be appointed by the Emperor.

The role of the ministers, all of whom are appointed and removable by the Emperor, needs no elaboration; ministerial functions are much the same in every country. However, it must be emphasized again that even so high a post as minister does not carry with it in Ethiopia the independence of judgment and action that it would in democratic states. Moreover, some ministers (notably in recent years Makonnen Habtewold, the Minister of Finance) appear to exercise far more influence throughout the government than their immediate powers and duties might suggest. Such special influence, usually the result of a minister's strong personal ties with the Emperor, has an atrophying effect on responsible administration.

Foreign advisers are employed in a number of ministries to do the work of organization and planning that is required. Their work entails many frustrations. Although their advice is continually sought, it is often not accepted; if it is accepted, it may be claimed by the minister as his own. The advisers find it hard to gain the confidence of the inner circles of Ethiopian administration, and often are not told what has become of their proposals. The policy of employing advisers from several different countries is still followed by the government, despite the difficulty of coordinating backgrounds and viewpoints, because of the traditional Amhara suspicion of possible domination by one foreign power.

Ministries exist for Agriculture, Commerce and Industry, Education,[6] Finance, Foreign Affairs, the Interior, Justice, Communications, Public Health, Public Works, and War. There is also a Ministry of the Pen, exercising such miscellaneous functions as keeping the Great Seal, the archives, and the vital statistics of the imperial family, issuing the *Negarit Gazeta,* coordinating the work of the other ministries, and supplying the official liaison with Parliament. The names of the ministries are sometimes altered, and occasionally a new one is added

[6] Because of his great interest in the subject, the Emperor serves as his own minister of education.

or an old one subdivided. Within each ministry there are departments, as well as smaller administrative divisions, all responsible to
the minister or vice-minister. These, in turn, are individually responsible to the Emperor, and not to the Prime Minister, as might be
surmised. The Prime Minister serves primarily as a liaison officer
between the Emperor and the ministers collectively, or between both
of these and Parliament.

There is little coordination between the various ministries and a
considerable jealousy among them, despite the frequent meetings of
the Council of Ministers. This lack of coordination is the despair of
Point Four personnel in Ethiopia. Projects of a pressing or urgent
nature, such as the expansion of electric-power production or the
development of an adequate urban water supply system, often remain
for several years under consideration.[7] In the end, when finally something must be done to avoid a complete breakdown, hasty and inadequate remedies are sought and so a more general solution is again
postponed. The theory seems to be that so long as the roof does not
actually leak it needs no repair. Of course, this theory has its adherents everywhere; moreover, the Ethiopian government is far from
wealthy, and a careful accounting of its limited resources must be
made. Still, it is hard to avoid the conclusion that the Ethiopians are
weak on planning and weaker still on execution.

Provincial administration in Ethiopia is organized along the following lines, as set forth in an imperial decree of August 27, 1942.[8]
The country is divided into twelve provinces,[9] which in turn are
divided into subprovinces, districts, and subdistricts. Governors of
provinces are appointed by the Emperor, are salaried, and are responsible to the various ministers of the Empire according to the nature
of the matter at hand. Most other provincial officials are also appointed
by the Emperor and not by their immediate superiors. The powers
of the governors are limited; they must give instructions to their

[7] As the result of the Emperor's personal initiative, resulting in a change
of management, an energetic and successful attack has lately been made on
both these problems.

[8] Administrative Regulations, Decree No. 1 of 1942.

[9] Eritrea is a separate "autonomous unit."

subordinates according to policies determined by the Ministry of the Interior, they are not to collect any but legally instituted taxes, and they are specifically not to accept the "gifts" formerly presented by the peasants to high officials.

The purpose of this decree, obviously, was to establish a firmly centralized administrative structure in place of the loose-knit system of favoritism and personal rule of old. The decree makes no mention of local self-government, or of the ancient office of *chica shum*, or village head, for centuries the central administration's immediate contact with the people. This traditional office continues to exist, but its exact relationship in the new scheme of things is not altogether clear. As previously stated, local and tribal institutions, such as the *gada* system of the Gallas, also survive in modified form within the general administrative framework of Amhara rule.

The governors exercise real authority over the people only through the *balabats,* the local tribal chiefs, who are the traditional leaders of the people. The *balabat* is the link through which the governor's authority descends to the peasants. If the governor has not succeeded in obtaining the good will and cooperation of this traditional figure, his administration may be rendered ineffective. Thus we see that, despite the attempt of the Amharas to impose a uniform and centralized bureaucratic system on the country, vastly different as it is from province to province, this system is able to function effectively only through cooperation with traditional and recognized tribal relationships.

Yet an over-all, centralized bureaucracy has been established and is functioning, and this alone represents a change of great significance in a country so recently divided and still composed of so many different elements. In time, by a slow process of education, by improved communications, by wider contact with the outside world, the people will presumably be brought to drop their outmoded sociopolitical forms, and the Amhara bureaucracy will become a genuine civil service, a system not merely superimposed on traditional ways of life but extending its services to every Ethiopian citizen.

In the realm of municipal government, the mayors of all municipalities except Addis Ababa are responsible to the governors of the provinces in which they are situated. The mayor of Addis Ababa answers to the Minister of the Interior. The mayors of Addis Ababa and Gondar are known as *kantibas*, and elsewhere as "officers of the town." They govern with the aid of a municipal council, composed in part of officials from the various ministries and in part of Ethiopian property owners in theory elected by other property owners. In fact, no Ethiopian approached by the author has ever witnessed such an election outside the capital, nor is there any provision in the law for the publication of electoral lists or anything else normally associated with elections. It appears that even in Addis Ababa the voting is on a very restricted basis, the participating electors being summoned by the Kantiba to a special meeting at which a choice of councilmen is made from a list previously nominated by the district officers. The whole procedure is conducted without publicity and normally without the knowledge of the general public. Decisions of the municipal council must be confirmed by the Minister of the Interior to have the force of law.

The municipal council is the legislative body of municipal government; the Kantiba or town officer exercises a largely executive function. It should be noted, however, that the Minister of the Interior has the supreme power over all municipal council decisions, and that none can enter into force without his approval. This again illustrates the Amhara leaders' passion for centralized control and their extreme distrust of any measure of local self-rule.

Only the larger communities in Ethiopia have any form of official municipal government. Most Ethiopians live in isolated settlements or clusters of huts on hilltops or where there are groups of trees, far from any road, and in too few numbers to warrant the establishment of any local administration. The many nomadic tribes have little contact with government officials. In the far south there are other isolated tribes, some still worshiping their own local "kings." Most Ethiopian "townships" consist merely of a few score grass or tin-roofed huts; they are colorless, shabby, without public facilities of any sort, forgetful of and all but forgotten by the world. They are governed, as they have been for centuries, by the *chica shum*, who is largely concerned with settling land disputes and is the purveyor of occasional orders from the governor of the province, the local *balabat*, or other officials.

The military will be touched upon only briefly here, because although it once formed the third leg of a triumvirate of which the other two were Church and State, it has nowhere near that importance today. The reason lies largely in the growing ascendancy of the political element in Ethiopian life during the last twenty-five years, especially since the restoration.

Up to the eve of Italian aggression in 1935, Ethiopia never had a professional army (except for the Imperial Guard and the Emperor's personal troops) comparable to what is understood by the term in Western lands. There were permanent garrisons in the southern provinces conquered by Menelik just before the turn of the century, but these lived a more or less settled local existence, engaged in no training, and were mostly soldiers in name only. The Emperor had a strong provincial army of his own, but so did each of his relations, and the governors and *rases* of the various provinces maintained their own forces. All these forces rarely trained, wore no uniforms to speak of, and were poorly armed. They could be called together by the Emperor in case of national emergency, as they were in 1935, in which case each governor was expected to provide his own troops, arm them, and lead them into battle. No satisfactory estimate could be made of the total number that could be mobilized at any moment, partly because of the difficulty of distinguishing fighting men from mere hangers-on (who also occasionally joined in the battle), partly because a general mobilization was so rarely called. They were a ragtail, barefoot lot (again with the exception of the Emperor's personal forces and the Imperial Guard) and certainly no match for the modern, mechanized Italian armies against which they were pitted in 1935.

After the liberation of Ethiopia by British and Commonwealth forces in 1941 a British military mission stayed behind, at the request of the Ethiopian government, "for the purpose of raising, organizing, and training the Ethiopian Army."[10] The Emperor also revived the Imperial Guard, in order to have a military force under his direct control. Swedish officers were subsequently employed to train this force, and other Swedes were hired to train the Air Force and the police. Prior to the war with Italy, Swiss and Belgian officers had been employed to train the Emperor's provincial soldiery, and in 1953, two years after the final withdrawal of the British mission, American training and military equipment were solicited. This lack of uniformity and continuity cannot but have its disadvantages, but it is apparently a price that the Ethiopians are willing to pay to assuage their fear of political domination by any one nation.

The British Military Mission to Ethiopia, as the British mission was officially called, at first had an executive character, necessitated by the fact that after the 1941 restoration the Ethiopian government was still in its formative stage. Later this executive role was spontaneously relinquished, and the mission's functions became advisory only. Its size was also progressively reduced, and in 1951 it withdrew altogether.

In addition to the forces trained by the British mission and those of the Emperor, there was still another army in the country following the liberation. Its members, known as Territorials, were the remnants of the armed patriot bands that had been roaming and looting the country in the ancient Ethiopian tradition after the defeat of the Italians. The idea behind organizing them into a loose government force was largely to check this brigandage. Some of them were subsequently absorbed into the regular army and their officers trained by the British mission; most of the others were enlisted into the newly formed national police.

It is impossible to ascertain the strength of the Ethiopian armed forces today. Secrecy surrounds the whole subject to a degree that is greater than usual in Ethiopia, and perhaps the answer is known to only the few directly concerned. Estimated budgetary expenditure for the Ministry of War, the Imperial Guard, and the Air Force in

---

[10] Article 2 of the military annex to the Anglo-Ethiopian Agreement, January 31, 1942.

1946 E.C. (Ethiopian Calendar)[11] was Eth.$26.5 million out of a total estimated ordinary expenditure of Eth.$100 million.[12] The Ethiopian Air Force consists of a few dozen outmoded propeller-driven planes that would be shot out of the sky within hours if a real war should start. The army, while better trained, clothed, and armed than it was in 1935, is almost certainly not larger than the 300,000-odd troops Ethiopia put into the field against Mussolini, although more than this number could perhaps be called to the colors in the event of a general conscription.

It would seem reasonable for Ethiopia to reduce her military expenditures sharply and divert the money saved into economically and socially more profitable channels. But, as in other countries, the military in Ethiopia is judged no longer solely from the standpoint of its contribution to defense, but from a political standpoint as well. It signifies prestige and power, important though intangible perquisites for a nation whose leaders are anxious to have the world sit up and take notice.

[11] Corresponding to the year ending September 10, 1954, Gregorian Calendar.

[12] The Ethiopian dollar has a par value of 40.25 cents in American money.

V

Public Finance

The concept that the ruler has the right to exact duties and tribute from his subjects for the support of government is one that has probably existed in all societies, even in those of the most rudimentary political development, from time immemorial. In Ethiopia, as already noted, tribute to the imperial house was for centuries based on the *gabar* system, a form of serfdom in which the peasants living on the land were required to surrender one-third or more of their produce to the landowner, often the Emperor himself or the Church, in addition to paying the traditional tithe and a host of petty taxes that have in recent years been largely abolished. The governors of the various provinces collected this tribute and sent it to the Emperor along with horses, lengths of cloth, and gold, after deducting their own "expenses" and the costs of provincial administration, including the upkeep of their private armies. There are no adequate data available on the total amount of this revenue accruing to the central government before 1935. Margery Perham has estimated that the total during the early 'thirties did not exceed £500,000 per year.[1] Even in the late 'thirties most of the revenue was in kind—very little (chiefly customs fees) in cash. Expenditure was correspondingly limited to a few municipal necessities, the support of the Emperor's household, and maintenance of the army.

This archaic system of receipts in kind, based more on custom

[1] *The Government of Ethiopia*, p. 195.

than on law, was, of course, incompatible with the modern fiscal system that was necessary after the 1941 restoration, if only to assure proper maintenance of the expensive road system and the many public buildings the Italians had constructed during their five-year occupation of the country.

The fiscal system as it exists today is largely a postwar product, although certain taxes based on ancient customs are still levied in some parts of the country. Some remote sections, in fact, still pay taxes in the old Maria Theresa thaler, which has been outlawed since 1945. Hoards of these thalers are without doubt still buried in the ground, along with many of the newer fifty-cent coins issued during and after the currency reform of that year. However, revenue from these sources is negligible, and for the purpose of the present study may safely be neglected.

Ethiopia's main source of revenue is the customs tax on imported goods, which was largely nonexistent in earlier times. Although certain duties were imposed on imports before the war with Italy, the present tariff system is the result of a thorough revision made shortly after the country's liberation, the work of a British adviser of long experience in the field, Mr. C. T. Underhill. The first revised customs schedule was published in the *Negarit Gazeta* of June 30, 1943; it has since been several times amended.

Ethiopia's tariff system is a mixed one, some rates being ad valorem while others are fixed at so much per unit or weight. Most export duties are on a weight basis. Some items are classed as duty-free. There are at present no direct trade controls, and aside from a few formal trade agreements of a very general nature, no restrictive agreements with other countries.[2]

The system may be described as fiscal, since its main purpose is to provide revenue rather than to protect local industry or prohibit certain classes of import. Aside from the various duty rates specified (which range from 10 per cent to 100 per cent) there are several special taxes of various sorts, as well as several provisions of law permitting

[2] Ethiopia is not a party to the General Agreement on Tariffs and Trade (GATT).

exemption from customs duties. The basic law of 1943 referred to above authorizes the Minister of Finance, with the consent of the Council of Ministers, to "grant total or partial exemption from the payment of duty on any goods which in the public interest should be granted such an exemption." A later proclamation, No. 145 of 1954, exempts from all import duties and taxes agricultural and industrial machines, implements, appliances, and parts thereof.

One of the special taxes levied and collected on imports is the federal tax of 10 per cent ad valorem introduced in 1954 to help finance the cost of federal expenditures in Ethiopia and Eritrea. Another is the federal tax on salt imposed for the same reason. A third is a 1 per cent levy on goods cleared through the customs at Addis Ababa and imposed by the municipal authorities of that city. There are, in addition, several minor fees and duties.

Duties are also levied on a few export items, of which the most important at present is coffee. Export duties, however, provide far less revenue than imports. With regard to coffee, the government has tended to adjust its tax to price fluctuations. A sliding scale surtax was introduced during the sharp price rise of 1954, resulting in a tax which was almost confiscatory of profits above a certain level. With the subsequent decline of coffee prices, both the fixed and the graduated surtaxes on this commodity were reduced, and the point at which the graduated tax came into operation was fixed at a lower level. In addition to the foregoing, a federal tax of 2 per cent ad valorem on all exports was introduced in 1954.

Normally customs duties on both exports and imports account for a little over 40 per cent of ordinary government revenue. They are the largest single source of this revenue. Next in importance as revenue producers are the so-called direct taxes, i.e., personal and business tax, land tax, cattle tax, education tax, tithe, and a few others. These comprise perhaps 33 per cent of the total. Indirect taxes (alcohol, tobacco, motor fuel, and toll taxes and the like) constitute about 12 per cent of total revenue,[3] with the balance made up of court fees,

---

[3] These taxes are not discussed in any detail here; the interested reader will find a complete description of them in an *Informative Bulletin* pub-

postal, telegraph, and telephone earnings, gold production, and other miscellaneous receipts and earnings of government departments.

The personal and business tax does not apply to income from agriculture or handicrafts, occupations that employ perhaps 90 per cent of the Ethiopian population. It is paid only by the small minority engaged in other pursuits, such as commerce or government service. Incomes up to Eth.$360 per annum are free of tax. (Average annual per capita income in Ethiopia is probably less than half this.) The rates are not high: a maximum of 15 per cent with a surtax of 10 per cent on any net income over Eth.$100,000. As noted earlier, however, assessment is often arbitrary, particularly with regard to businesses that cannot produce accurate accounting records.

The land tax now levied is, like most other taxes, a development of the postwar period. As already indicated, land taxes prior to 1935 were collected according to old customs and were mainly in kind, i.e, in cereals or in services. This whole system was swept away by Land Tax Proclamation No. 8 of 1942, which was in turn superseded in 1944 by a new proclamation. Together with numerous amendments and additional regulations since introduced, today's law provides, in contrast to the old semifeudal system of uncertain levies, for fixed rates per unit of land according to its fertility. The land unit is the *gasha*, an ill-defined measure ranging between 80 and 100 acres. The system is not uniform in all parts of the country, and there are still some lands to which special privileges attach. The tithe, formerly a flexible tax representing a tenth of the produce of the land, was altered by the 1944 law to a fixed basis. Some lands, among them those of the Church, are exempt from the land tax but are required to pay a tax in lieu of tithe.

Aside from the land tax and tithe, an education tax on land is levied for the support of elementary education in the province where the tax is collected. This tax is similarly levied per *gasha* and varies

---

lished by the Ministry of Finance of the Imperial Ethiopian Government in February 1955, and available from that ministry at Eth.$1.00 per copy.

It should be added that the account in these pages of taxes levied and collected in Ethiopia does not apply in all respects to Eritrea. The differences are touched upon in Chapter X.

according to the land's assessed fertility. It is not uniform throughout the country, but there are apparently no privileged lands exempt from the payment of this tax. There is also a tax on cattle and other live-stock, at fixed rates per animal, payable by the nomadic population who do not pay land tax.

In addition to revenue from taxation, the Ethiopian government derives a certain income from public utilities (including the postal service); from its gold mines, particularly at Adola (Kebre Menghist) in the south; and from its share in the profits of enterprises in which it has invested capital (such as the State Bank) or otherwise obtained an interest. Income from these sources accounts for between 15 and 20 per cent of what is termed in the Ethiopian budget "Ordinary Revenue," plus capital profits.

Ethiopia actually has two budgets: the ordinary budget, which covers normal revenues and expenditures, and the extraordinary budget, which covers special items such as loan receipts and repayments and other large capital outlays. This statement must be immediately qualified, however, by saying that these "budgets" bear little relation to what is understood by the term in advanced countries. In actual fact, the government since the end of the war has been operating by "budgetary decision" and not on the basis of a fixed budget. That is, there has been no preplanned schedule of revenue and expenditure as a whole. Funds have been dispersed as requests for them, submitted by the various government ministries, have been approved by the Council of Ministers. The practice has been automatically to renew an appropriation from year to year unless a new request is received. Estimates of revenues and expenditures, usually made a year or more after the event by the Ministry of Finance, are termed the "budget." The framing of a proper budget for the fiscal year to come is supposed to be a responsibility of Parliament, but once again practice is far from theory.[4]

[4] The revised constitution of 1955 specifically states that a draft budget shall be submitted to and approved by Parliament at least one month before the beginning of the new fiscal year. Before this can be done it appears that a major reorganization in accounting as well as in administrative procedures will be required.

The budgetary policy of the government has always been very conservative. Despite a number of deficit years in the past, a cash surplus has been maintained from which the occasional deficits have been financed. The main items of expenditure, as well as the main sources of revenue, occur in the ordinary budget; the outlays are confined to salaries and other administrative costs of running the government departments. Almost all expenses, with the exception of the public debt, are entered in the budget under the headings of the various ministries and departments. For example, almost the whole cost of provincial administration appears as an expenditure under the Ministry of the Interior.

Revenues and expenditures of the Ethiopian government in 1956 were each in the neighborhood of Eth.$100 million a year, against approximately half that amount at the close of the war in 1945. In 1958 they were estimated as running close to Eth.$140 million. This will give some idea of the prosperity and growth that the country has experienced in the first postwar decade, largely as the result of a favorable market for its chief export, coffee.

The largest single item of expenditure in the ordinary budget is the Ministry of the Interior, with approximately 15 per cent of the total; second is the Ministry of War, with 14 per cent; third, the Ministry of Education, with 11 per cent. Add expenditures for the Imperial Guard, the Air Force, the police, and prisons to those of the Ministry of War, and it becomes apparent that over 35 per cent of the total ordinary expenditure of the government goes for defense and the maintenance of law and order. As against this, the listed cost of provincial administration (excluding Eritrea) is less than 7 per cent of the total, road building is 8 per cent, and the expenditure for the development of agriculture—the country's basic economic activity—including contributions to FAO and Point Four, is a mere 1 per cent of the total.

Certainly the agriculture budget is far too small. Ten or even fifteen times this amount could with profit be spent on development in this field, on which the future progress of the country largely depends. Experiment stations could be built, state farms organized, better tools and better seed distributed to the peasants, improved farming methods introduced, cooperative ventures supported and encouraged, extension services organized, and the expanded cultivation of economically important crops, such as cotton, vigorously pushed. Related expenditures on education and on communications, in particular roads, could be substantially increased without any immediate danger of surpassing the optimum level. But the will to organize and to improve agriculture on a sufficient scale appears to be numbed. No Minister of Agriculture so far has had the enterprise, imagination, and will to make of his ministry the important factor that it could and should be in the economic development of the country.

The problem goes deeper than the mere choice of a minister. The Amhara ruling class in general seems unwilling to forsake the sedentary bureaucratic life of the capital and the Western amenities to which it has there become accustomed; it is content to leave its numerous rural holdings in the hands of ignorant overseers, who know nothing of scientific farming or management. The cultivated Amhara shrinks from physical labor, and especially from soiling his hands. Little progress can be expected, in agriculture or elsewhere, while such attitudes prevail.

Road-building expenditures, too, are insufficient if the people of the interior are to be introduced, by sight and personal acquaintance, to better clothing, shoes, houses, sanitary facilities, and simple farm and household implements. Feeder roads need to be built off the main highways to open up the country. But again, imagination, organization, and enterprise are needed at the top; these roads will not get built as long as the government is content to adopt grandiose plans that are forever being changed or postponed.[5]

A considerable proportion (approximately 11 per cent) of public funds is currently devoted to education. Expenditures here could also very well be increased, partly to permit more school-age children to attend school, partly to improve the quality of education for a

[5] Recently (1957) a new highway improvement program was initiated with the help of a $15 million loan from the International Bank for Reconstruction and Development, which should go a considerable way toward meeting the need.

smaller number of promising students, perhaps by sending a larger number of qualified young men abroad and for a longer period. Here again it is not capital so much that Ethiopia needs, but the services of a self-reliant, enterprising, and imaginative leadership that is able to rise above the debilitating influences of the society from which it has sprung. Those who have had the benefit of an education must become the leaven for those who have not.

The extraordinary budget, as indicated, is concerned mainly with foreign loans and with other capital items. Of foreign aid there has been a substantial amount since 1941, ranging all the way from the British subsidies of the early years to the IBRD loans of the later postwar period. A British grant of £3,250,000 was of considerable help in restoring the impoverished finances of the regime between 1942 and 1945. There followed aid from the United States in the form of lend-lease equipment and supplies to the value of approximately U.S.$5,000,000 (including thirty million Ethiopian silver fifty-cent coins which had been minted in the United States). A Swedish loan of 5,000,000 kroner was extended to Ethiopia in 1945 to facilitate salary transfers of Swedes employed in Ethiopia and to purchase school and hospital equipment in Sweden. This was raised to 7,500,000 kroner the following year. In the same year, 1946, the United States extended to Ethiopia a credit of U.S.$500,000, later increased to U.S.$1,000,000, to finance the purchase of war surplus stocks. The Export-Import Bank of Washington also supplied a U.S.$500,000 loan in the closing days of 1944 (repaid in full by 1946) and a line of credit of U.S.$3,000,000 in 1946, the last to finance the purchase of a variety of items, including automobiles and trucks, industrial machinery, gold-mining equipment, educational supplies, and currency notes and coins. A U.S.$900,000 National City Bank credit of 1947, used to finance the manufacture and shipment of additional Ethiopian fifty-cent coins, was liquidated the same year. In August 1948, and again in October 1949, Ethiopia availed herself of her membership in the International Monetary Fund to purchase a total of U.S.$600,000 for an equivalent sum in her own currency. Both transactions were made to alleviate a hard currency shortage existing at the time. In 1950 and 1951 came three development loans from the International Bank, which will be described in some detail in Chapter IX, and a private American credit of U.S.$324,000 to help finance the purchase by Ethiopian Airlines, Inc., the country's national airline, of two Convair passenger planes.

The three IBRD loans of 1950 and 1951 have played an important role in Ethiopia's economic rehabilitation and expansion. Together they totaled U.S.$8,500,000 — $5,000,000 for the rehabilitation and maintenance of the country's main road network, $2,000,000 for the establishment of a bank to make small loans to agriculture and industry, and $1,500,000 for the improvement and extension of the telecommunications system. The highway loan had been utilized in full by the end of May, 1954; it was administered by a special highway authority, whose management was chosen by the Ethiopian government in cooperation with the International Bank. A similar board was established under the telecommunications loan. A new lending institution, the Ethiopian Development Bank, was organized under the third loan, absorbing in the process the previously existing Agricultural and Commercial Bank of Ethiopia. Repayments on the three loans, all of which bear interest at 3 per cent plus 1 per cent commission, began in 1956.

The Ethiopian government has had a good record in meeting interest and principal repayments on all of its foreign obligations of the postwar period. The total foreign indebtedness outstanding at the end of 1955 was Eth.$28.1 million, of which about 65 per cent was to the IBRD. As a measure of the government's sound financial position it may be pointed out that on the same date the free foreign reserves of the central bank, the State Bank of Ethiopia, amounted to almost twice the country's external debt.

Largely as a result of this favorable performance record, the IBRD on June 28, 1957, concluded a further loan agreement with the Ethiopian government (in which the First National City Bank of New York is participating), under which an additional $15 million will be provided by the World Bank to finance part of the foreign exchange cost of extension and improvement of Ethiopia's highway system. As was the case with the first highway loan, the Ethiopian government will participate in this new program with the appropriation of much larger funds of its own.

Also reflecting confidence in Ethiopia's credit record was the action of the Export-Import Bank of Washington on November 26, 1957, in extending to that country a new line of credit of $24 million, for the construction, improvement, and enlargement of its aviation facilities.

Also in 1957, the Ethiopian government signed a contract with a Yugoslav firm for the construction of modern docking facilities at the port of Assab, the southernmost of Ethiopia's two outlets on the Red Sea, at a cost of Eth.$26 million, half of which was to be advanced by the construction company at 3 per cent interest.

That these later loans were far larger than any of the earlier ones reflects a widespread confidence in Ethiopia's present and future economic position. It seems likely that they will be quite within the country's ability to manage.

Apart from foreign loans, so-called extraordinary revenue is also realized on occasion by the "sale" of the government's promissory notes to the State Bank, from the issue of coins, and from profits on the government's capital investments.

The sale of promissory notes to the State Bank can take place only when there is a surplus, or an excess, of foreign reserves in the bank's Issue Department above the 30 per cent minimum required by law as backing for the outstanding issue of Ethiopian currency notes. According to a 1950 amendment to the 1945 Currency and Legal Tender Proclamation, the basic currency law of the country, there must at all times exist a backing of 100 per cent for Ethiopian currency notes, consisting of a minimum of 30 per cent in gold, silver, and foreign assets (foreign balances and foreign securities) and a maximum of 70 per cent in so-called "Treasury Bills" issued by the Ethiopian government. The latter are in theory themselves secured by a pledge of 110 per cent of the fixed assets of the government. What these fixed assets are, however, has never been defined, nor has the manner in which they could, if necessary, be realized. Treasury bills are, in fact, nothing more than an inflationary device by which the government can convert "excess" foreign reserves into Ethiopian dollar deposits with the State Bank, which handles all the government's accounts. Revenue so obtained is in the nature of a forced, non-interest-bearing, nonrepayable "loan," if the term can be applied at all.

A similar situation occurs when extraordinary revenue is obtained through the issuance of new coins. The cost of manufacturing coins is borne by the government, in contrast to the cost of manufacturing banknotes, which is borne by the State Bank. (Both banknotes and coins are produced in the United States.) When coins are issued, the government is credited on its accounts with the central bank with the face value of the coins, thus realizing a profit on the difference between this value and the cost of manufacture and shipment to Ethiopia. This revenue, unlike that obtained from the issuance of Treasury Bills, is not under the direct control of the government, occurring more or less incidentally as coins are released in accordance with the needs of trade. But this source of revenue is not very important from year to year, whereas the revenue from Treasury Bills can be very substantial (e.g., Eth.$25 million in 1956).

Profits of government-owned but self-operating enterprises, such as the State Bank, Ethiopian Airlines, Ethiopian Electric Light and Power, and the Imperial Ethiopian Tobacco Monopoly, whether reinvested or not, are another significant source of extraordinary revenue. Small amounts are sometimes also realized through the sale of state assets.

When we turn to "extraordinary expenditure" we find much the same breakdown of budgetary items that we found in considering extraordinary revenue. Among them are disbursements under foreign loans, expenditures for the printing of banknotes and the minting of coins, and accumulated and reinvested profits of government enterprises. Others, equally of a self-explanatory nature, consist of expenditures for capital works and investments and the subscription of capital for specific government enterprises, such as the Development Bank. Rather inconsistently, capital expenditures of the Imperial Highway Authority are listed in the ordinary budget. A curious item to be found in the extraordinary expenditures is the loss suffered by the State Bank on its sterling holdings in the 1949 currency devaluations (Ethiopia did not devalue). Since the State Bank is treated as an autonomous unit of the government in the revenue side of the budget, only its net earnings being considered, this devaluation entry would seem to be another inconsistency in accounting procedure.

Income from the government's gold mines has never been an important source of revenue. Gold-mining machinery, purchased in 1951 with a part of the proceeds of the 1946 Export-Import Bank credit referred to above, was hailed by some as heralding a large increase in production, but this has not materialized. Gold production has remained at the level of a few thousand ounces yearly since the end of World War II. The mechanization, it has been charged, was never allowed to come into effective operation by certain highly placed Ethiopian officials with a direct interest in preserving the present loosely controlled system of placer mining. It is a fact that difficulties of all sorts plagued the project: spare parts were never in adequate supply, organizational troubles arose, and little or no cooperation was given the American chief mining engineer by the Minister of Finance and other government officials. In October 1953, in an attempt to rescue the operation, an Imperial Ethiopian Mining Board was set up, with a capital of Eth.$2,000,000, under the chairmanship of the Minister of Finance, Makonnen Habtewold. It was from the beginning apparent that Habtewold was at best lukewarm about the whole project. As a result of his indifference or obstructionism the board never really came into effective operation, and less than two years after its establishment it was dissolved on the recommendation of its members.

No one knows how much gold there actually is in Ethiopia, or how important it could be as a source of revenue if properly developed. No adequate surveys have been made. The same applies to other minerals. Oil production, a potentially large revenue producer if explorations should ever prove successful, is similarly a question mark. The Sinclair Petroleum Company pulled up its stakes in early 1957 after some ten years of effort and a capital investment of approximately $10 million, which succeeded in producing only dry holes.

Barring some such spectacular development as the finding of oil, which now seems extremely doubtful, Ethiopian government revenues will continue to depend largely on the sources already mentioned, and in particular on customs duties. Fluctuations in coffee prices and production will be dominant in this regard, in view of the major importance of this commodity, which accounts for well over 50 per cent, in value, of Ethiopian exports in good years. We come back, therefore, to the conclusion that improved agricultural output, leading to increased exports, is the key to Ethiopia's future.

VI

Agriculture

The Ethiopian economy is primarily agricultural, the country possessing natural advantages in this sphere which could some day make it the breadbasket of the Middle East. The climate is mostly favorable, the soil good, and the rainfall sufficient to support, in general, a year-round growing season. With proper leadership and organization Ethiopia has ahead of her a great agricultural potential.

Yet far too little emphasis is placed on this promising aspect of Ethiopian development. Educated Amharas seem to feel that physical labor is degrading.[1] The Amhara landowner prefers to hire an overseer to manage his absentee holdings, and even some native agricultural students have been criticized[2] for their reluctance to sully their hands. In fairness, however, it must be said that the government has been cooperating with the U.S. Point Four technicians in the setting up of an agricultural technical school, which is now in full operation and in July, 1957, graduated eleven Ethiopian boys with B.S. degrees in General Agriculture. An increasing number of such graduates in the years ahead should prove to be an important factor in the development of Ethiopian agriculture.

Rapid industrialization is just not yet in the cards in the present

[1] Menial physical labor has in Ethiopia traditionally been performed by the Gurage people, whom it was in former times the custom to summon from the street by the cry of "Gurage! Gurage!" This is now taboo, and the cry of "Coolie! Coolie!" is most often heard instead.

[2] In private remarks to the author by a former FAO Chief of Mission.

state of the Ethiopian economy and society. An industralized nation requires at least a literate population, urbanized social groups responsive to monetary incentives, skilled and semiskilled workers, a managerial class, and a sizable internal market for the products of industry. Industrialization also requires large capital outlays and a capital market (unless all investment is from abroad), adequate roads, communications, and housing, a general willingness to regularize social relationships according to law and contract, and a more or less homogeneous feeling of nationhood. None of these requirements is yet met in Ethiopia except in limited degree, and the outlook for rapid change in these directions is not promising.

These considerations should be kept in mind when an analysis of the Ethiopian economy is attempted. Agriculture is—and will for long remain—the dominant theme. The Ethiopian people are, for the most part, bound to the soil, or to their herds, and this is where the main emphasis on future development must be laid.

In an earlier chapter it was noted that approximately 9 per cent of the land area of the country is arable and some 30 per cent is pastoral. Although some arable land is to be found almost everywhere, the heaviest concentration of such land is in the northern highlands, the traditional home of the Ethiopian people. Other arable land areas include parts of the southern and southeastern slopes and the Rift Valley along the Awash River. Erosion is very heavy and has been going on for centuries. Little, if anything, is being done about it.

The sowing and harvesting of crops is carried on in the most primitive manner and with the simplest kind of agricultural implements. Ethiopian agriculture is mainly a subsistence agriculture, the Ethiopian farmer selling only about 10 to 20 per cent of his produce. Crop yields are very low, despite generally good soil, owing to the crude farming methods employed. After sowing, for instance, and when the crop has started to grow, it is usual to plow over the land again to eliminate weeds; this practice uproots a great many young plants at the same time, and is thus wasteful and inefficient. The Ethiopian farmer is not acquainted with row seeding. The practice is to broadcast the seeds onto the bare ground, letting them fall where they may and then plowing them over. This makes the use of a hoe for cultivation difficult.

The Ethiopian plow is a crude instrument, being mainly a digging tool. It does not turn the soil, but merely breaks it, so that plowing must be repeated three or four times before an adequate seedbed can be formed. Plowing is generally done on wet soil, since the hard sun-baked clay soil of Ethiopia offers too much resistance to the light Ethiopian plow. These plows are generally made of wood with a steel point, the wooden parts being fashioned by the farmer himself. They are simple and cheap to make and very light, but have the disadvantage of very slow and poor performance, so that plowing is the most expensive item in farming. Their useful life is short. They turn up ground roughly, leaving big clods and causing an irregular growth of seeds.

Mechanical sources of traction are virtually unknown in Ethiopia, except on a few scattered European-run concessions. Nor are horses used as draft animals, although the Ethiopian horse is plentiful and strong enough for traction. Wheeled transport is likewise virtually unknown; instead donkeys, camels, horses, or mules are used as pack animals. As mentioned earlier, this arrangement is far from efficient; a simple cart drawn by a horse could do the work of ten pack donkeys. Such a cart could be easily made by the farmer himself; persuading him to make one is another matter. As one FAO expert observed in his official report to the Ethiopian government: "The introduction of new tools is . . . largely a question of education."

Most of the tools used by the Ethiopian farmer are made of old scrap iron, which is not very well hardened, so that the cutting edges are not resistant. The wooden parts are made chiefly of hard wood. Tools are never sharpened, although there are many sources of good sandstones. Spades are used for breaking up pasture land. In the south, the 'spade' is usually only a sharp wooden stick; in the north it is sometimes a stick with two iron points. The hoe is useful, but under the system of broadcast planting, the weeds often grow faster than hoeing can be done. Several types of crude sickles and hatchets are used, but the scythe—a far more efficient instrument than the sickle—is unknown.

Threshing is usually done by oxen trampling the outspread sheaves until the grain falls out. Wooden shovels and forks are then used to toss the grain into the wind in order to separate the chaff from the grain. A further cleaning operation is then performed with sieves and bowls. The final product is short of the standard demanded by the international market; up to 15 per cent of it may be straw, weeds, manure, and dirt. Moreover, certain undesirable combinations (such as soft and hard wheat in a wheat sample) often render the grain, if not unsalable, most unattractive to discriminating buyers. With regard to wheat, "It is not uncommon to see hard, soft, bearded, beardless, white, red, and purple varieties growing in the same field."[3] Cleaning and grading (required by law since 1950 for grain intended for sale on the export market) will remove most of the weed seeds and inert matter, but grain varieties cannot normally be separated by mechanical means.

The Ethiopian farmer stores his grain in receptacles made of mud-plastered wickerwork. Loss due to rodents is extremely high. The processing of grain products is done either in wooden mortars or in a stone mill, and in general food preparation is very primitive. The mill used consists of a bottom stone and a much smaller runner stone, which grinds the grain until the desired fineness is reached. Production is about two pounds per hour. This work is very slow and exhausting and is done mostly by women.

One of FAO's recommendations to the Ethiopian government was that a light, simple, and inexpensive type of moldboard plow be substituted for the traditional Ethiopian plow. This would permit the plowing of twice, and even of three times, as much land per hour as the Ethiopian plow, and because of the moldboard its performance under dry conditions and in heavy soils would be good. Such plows, experimentally produced and tried by FAO, were also satisfactory in breaking up virgin soils, making use of a spade unnecessary. Once again, the problem has been getting Ethiopian farmers to use the new equipment. An FAO report on small agricultural tools[4] made the following comment on the approximately Eth.$1 million worth of plows and agricultural equipment donated to Ethiopia in 1945 by the United Nations Relief and Rehabilitation Administration (UNRRA),

[3] FAO Report on Seed Improvement to the Government of Ethiopia, No. 191 (Rome, November 1953).

[4] No. 194 (Rome, October 1953).

and rusting away since then in government sheds on the outskirts of
Addis Ababa: "To leave unused, or use incorrectly, the UNRRA material stored by the government is to relinguish, voluntarily, an opportunity of improving Ethiopian farming conditions." Some of this
material has apparently been distributed, and some is not well adapted
to Ethiopian conditions, but most remains stored in the government
warehouse. The same expert writes that "contrary to general opinion,
the UNRRA plows are suitable for use under heavy soil conditions."
Nevertheless, since they are more complicated than what the Ethiopian farmer has been used to, he suggested that a start be made with
an experimental moldboard plow that could be produced locally at
very little cost, and which many Addis Ababa firms expressed willingness to exchange for the UNRRA plows. These recommendations
were made in 1953; the Ethiopian government has not yet taken any
action on them. The UNRRA equipment continues to deteriorate,
unused, at Akaki, a lesson to those who are inclined to assert that all
that underdeveloped countries need is capital.

The FAO report on small agricultural tools also recommended introduction of the scythe to replace the sickle; the use of light, hand-
operated threshers in place of the obsolete system of threshing by oxen;
the use of the horse for traction and for drawing small carts; the improved cleaning and grading of cereals; and the setting up, by the
Ministry of Agriculture, of training centers to instruct farmers in the
use of small tools. As far as is known, none of these recommendations
has yet been carried out.

The most widely grown food crop in the highlands is *teff* (*Eragros-
tis abyssinica*), a very fine grain cereal of the lovegrass variety. This
forms one of the staples of the Ethiopian diet, but little is exported,
since there is virtually no demand for it elsewhere. Other grains,
among them barley, wheat, and maize, are also grown, along with a
type of sorghum known locally as *dhurra*. Coffee is an important
crop for export, and is also consumed in some quantity by the Ethiopians. *Teff* and wheat are the popular bread grains, while barley is
normally used as a feed stock. Little cotton is grown, although there
are some indications to suggest that it would thrive, and it would un-

questionably fill a pressing economic need. Vegetables and fruits are not nearly as widely raised as in Europe or America. Oilseeds, however, are extensively produced both for export and for domestic use.

It is difficult to describe the various crops grown in terms of specific growing areas because of the wide variations in land elevation to be found throughout the country. Some crops can be grown very generally; others are confined to specific areas depending on the altitude or rainfall. The small grains are more commonly grown on the higher elevations; maize, grain sorghums, and *teff* thrive at medium altitudes; cotton grows somewhat lower. Aside from the main crops mentioned, a considerable variety of minor crops are also grown in Ethiopia, but these are of no great commercial importance. The wide variation of soil and climate in Ethiopia, combined with a generally adequate rainfall, makes it possible to raise successfully almost any type of crop with proper care and cultivation.

From the standpoint of cash crops, coffee is by far the most important. The total production, like that of other produce, is unknown, but some 42,000 tons were exported in 1955,[5] bringing in Eth.$90.2 million of foreign exchange and comprising 55.6 per cent of the total value of Ethiopia's exports. The Ethiopian coffee is all of the "arabica," or mocha, variety, which is found chiefly at high altitudes. Because of the resemblance of the word coffee to the name of the Ethiopian province of Kaffa, some maintain that this province in the western part of the country is the legendary home of coffee; unhappily for this hypothesis, the Ethiopian word for coffee is *buna*. Coffee arabica may be indigenous to Ethiopia; in any event, it has been grown there for centuries. It is produced in large part under "wild" conditions (i.e., in untended coffee forests) and in part on small native plots, often alongside other crops, and with little or no care after the seedling is once planted. A few larger plantations—some operated by Europeans, one by the Ethiopian government—produce a small crop. For the rest, coffee production is small, individual, haphazard, or "wild."

Ethiopian coffee beans are of high quality and excellent coffee can be made from them, as proved when beans properly picked and pre-

---

[5] Less than 2 per cent of world output.

pared by the "wet" method were tested by an expert coffee liquorer under FAO auspices. However, Ethiopian methods of preparation result in a poor product, unreliable and never uniform in quality. The coffee has a tendency to be sour, to ferment, and to have an earthy taste. The coffee cleaning and grading regulations of the government have not overcome these deficiencies, although they have resulted in a product of better appearance and size uniformity.

In most districts the trees are picked only once a year, regardless of whether the berries collected are ripe, green, or dried. Later, fallen berries which have rotted on the ground are collected. The berries are then imperfectly dried on the earth and after a few days are taken to a mill for hulling or are processed at home with flails, stones, pieces of wood, or pestles and mortars. No efforts are made to prevent the beans from becoming wet in transit, and no care is taken to keep the beans separate from materials which might give them a bad odor or flavor.

FAO has in this field, too, made a number of carefully thought out recommendations to the Ethiopian government, which include the following: (1) Creating a "coffee board," along the lines of the Brazilian Coffee Institute or the native coffee boards of Tanganyika, to coordinate all aspects of the production, processing, and marketing of coffee. (2) Setting up coffee settlement centers on government lands suitable for coffee, at which farmers can be instructed in the best methods of production and preparation. (3) Enlarging the coffee research program of the Jimma Agricultural Technical School, whose research program was described in the school's 1954 annual report[6] as "a drop in the bucket," to which only one part-time person was contributing. Since then, however, it appears that the program has been greatly enlarged, with some half million seedlings planted under the direction of two coffee experts by the end of 1955. (4) Establishing standard types, based upon the green bean, roast, and cup characteristics of coffees from various districts, the separation of "washed" from "nat-

[6] *The Agriculture of Ethiopia* (January 1954), I, 54. Report of staff—Imperial Ethiopian College of Agricultural and Mechanical Arts and Jimma Agricultural Technical School.

ural" coffee prepared by the dry method, and the blending of coffee from different districts to produce named types. (5) Setting up an extension program with a view to gradually transforming the coffee forests into efficient plantations by regulating shade and density of trees, removing competing underbrush, establishing seedling nurseries, and increasing the quality of beans by improving picking and drying methods. (6) Improving roads to coffee districts, now often isolated and difficult of access. These recommendations were made in May 1955; except for road improvement, no news of any government action on them has come to the attention of the writer.[7]

Another of the problems of Ethiopian agriculture is seed improvement. For centuries Ethiopian peasants have been planting with inferior seed, of mixed types, and obtaining yields at least 20 per cent below what could be obtained with superior seed. The production and distribution of high-quality seeds—either by private enterprise or by government plant-breeding stations—has not been hard to organize in other countries, but no movement to this end has made any headway in Ethiopia. The country's so-called "model farms" are nothing more than government lands leased out to local farmers. No experimental work is done (except in cross-breeding sheep and cattle at one or two places).

All the FAO reports and the Point Four reports speak of the need for experiment stations. Specifically, the FAO expert who reported on seed improvement in November 1953 recommended to the government "the organization within the Ministry of Agriculture of a section to deal with the introduction, production, and distribution of pure seeds and the administration and management of experiment farms," the "necessary provision of funds within the budget of the Ministry of Agriculture for the operation of experiment farms," the employment of qualified technicians, the training of personnel, and the use of UNRRA and unused Italian machinery in seed production. (At present, Ethiopian growers must rely on imported seeds, since there is no production of pure Ethiopian seed.) As an example of the

[7] The Ethiopian Development Bank, however, has for some time been granting small loans for the clearing, planting, and pruning of wild coffee forests, and has helped finance a coffee-processing center near Jimma, which uses the "wet" method, chiefly for demonstration purposes.

bottlenecks to be overcome, typifying the traditional Amhara reluctance to delegate authority, the FAO expert cites in his report the fact that in the absence of a section in the Ministry of Agriculture responsible for the planting of an experimental area at Holetta, some twenty miles from the capital, many small problems had to be referred to the Minister or the Vice-Minister of Agriculture.

It is generally agreed that substantially higher yields of greater uniformity could be obtained in Ethiopian agriculture with the use of better seeds obtained from abroad, by selection among domestic plant populations, or by plant breeding. In this sphere FAO has recommended that the government assume responsibility for an adequate supply and distribution of pure seeds and that it concentrate, at least initially, on the first two of the three suggested methods of seed improvement, since plant breeding is a long-term project. FAO has also suggested the establishment of a central experiment station with local or branch stations for seed testing. This central station would conduct variety performance trials with improved seeds to find the most suitable, and could also be used as a demonstration area to create interest and demand among the farmers. The most suitable varieties of seed could then be multiplied, after cleaning and testing, by selected farmers under supervised growing conditions, and the resulting seed collected for sale to other farmers, after certification of grade and remuneration to growers.

The chief difficulty in implementing these relatively simple recommendations is again one of organization and education. It is not enough—although it would be a great step forward—to supply pure seed. The peasant must also desire to use it. In societies where wealth is based on the number of head of cattle owned or the amount of land held, the incentive to increase production is severely limited by the small number of ways in which a larger income can be spent. As Professor W. Arthur Lewis has pointed out, in underdeveloped societies the recipient of a sudden increase in income *would not know what to do with the extra money.*[8] His wants are so limited, and the standard of living all around him so low, that the desire to accumulate manufactured products for use or for ostentatious display, both of

[8] *The Theory of Economic Growth* (London, 1955), p. 30.

which motives are important driving forces in economically advanced countries, seldom arises. These motivations develop only slowly, as the peasant learns to imitate the higher cultures and materially more advanced standards of living with which he occasionally comes in contact.

As often as not, the Ethiopian's extra cash goes into the ground, not to the market. Hoarding has always been a strong compulsion among Ethiopians, and still exists. As mentioned earlier, there are still many millions of old silver Maria Theresa thalers buried all over Ethiopia, and silver fifty-cent coins issued after the currency reform of 1945 are apparently also being hoarded. Though there are some 45 million of these coins nominally in circulation within the country, among a population of perhaps 12 million men, women, and children, it is seldom that one ever sees one of them. Some are held as cash by the banks, of course, but there is little doubt that a great many of them lie buried in the ground.

The question of breaking this habit of hoarding and thereby stimulating demand is directly one of education, of the slow changing of a people's mores and social institutions. The difficulty of achieving such a change has already been discussed, but it crops up here once again as an underlying reason for the slowness of advance along the agricultural front. The old saying "You can lead a horse to water, but you can't make him drink" applies with especial force to the problem of creating demand in backward countries. The foreign technical experts in Ethiopia can only advise, suggest, or recommend. Whether, and to what extent, their recommendations are acted upon by the Ethiopian government is at least partly a question of aims, social forces, traditional ways of thinking, and of intangible qualities of initiative, enterprise, and organizing ability.

Since much of the land in Ethiopia is owned by the government, the Church, and a few wealthy absentee landlords, the prospects for agricultural reform would seem bright at first glance—merely a matter of winning over a dozen key people, and they among the best educated in the country. Unfortunately, the problem is much more complex. The Church, rock of conservatism and the status quo, finds little appeal in the economic incentives of which we have spoken, and progress is likely to be slowest of all here—slower, even, than on lands worked by individual peasant proprietors. The government is, at least on the surface, willing to make some improvements. Its efficiency as an administrative machine is limited, however, by the meager education and highly conservative orientation of its officials. The landlords, as we have seen, are simply not interested; they prefer to devote their energies and their capital to the relative amenities of urban life. The individual contribution they and they alone could make by virtue of their superior knowledge and incentives goes unmade. If not quite content with the superior income to which they have attained, they at least do not possess sufficient incentive to foresake the towns for the land. And there is no middle class with management ability or sufficient education to do the job for them.

One of the potentially great agricultural advances in Ethiopia could be the growing of cotton on a large scale. Although much experimental work remains to be done, some surveys suggest that many areas of the country are suitable for cotton, and there is no doubt that there exists a large consumer market for finished textiles. However, in this sphere, as in so many others, the same social and political, and to some extent economic, factors have inhibited the setting in motion of an adequate program.[9]

Cotton is of ancient origin in Ethiopia. There exists in the country an old and important cottage craft industry in spinning and weaving on a family basis. Most of the cotton now produced in Ethiopia (a few thousand bales annually) is consumed by this industry. The country must import raw cotton to supply the requirements of its three textile mills, at Asmara, Dire Dawa, and Addis Ababa. In addition, more than a third of Ethiopia's total imports each year consists of finished textiles, most of which could be locally produced if domestic output of raw cotton were adequate. It has been estimated that, without seriously interfering with the production of sorghums or other food crops, Ethiopia could devote two to three million acres to cotton growing and could hope to produce, on a long-term basis, as

[9] In 1956 there was considerable foreign interest in the possibility of large-scale cotton production in Ethiopia. Early in 1957 a private Indian firm entered into negotiations with the Ethiopian government with a view to erecting a 14,000-spindle, 300-loom cotton textile factory, with a capitalization of Eth.$6 million.

much as 400,000 bales of cotton annually. Among the economic factors which principally hinder efforts to develop cotton production on a large scale are insufficient capital, poor roads, lack of technical and commercial services, the low standard of agriculture in general, and the lack of reliable agricultural data, especially on cotton. The Italians made the first intensive studies of Ethiopia's cotton-growing possibilities during their occupation of the country. They established five main growing regions, each with a center for ginning and baling. A system of cotton concessions and districts was introduced over the whole country, and a semiofficial concern was created in an attempt to organize the cotton industry. Today very little remains of these efforts. Almost all the machinery has disappeared and all the cotton experimental farms and plots have been abandoned.

The FAO expert who reported to the Ethiopian government on cotton potentialities in 1955 lamented, among other things, that the peasant had chosen to "buy goods for immediate consumption or to invest in unproductive capital in the form of cattle, so that the surplus with which he started is wiped out without there ever being any question of the kind of investment which yields returns, such as land improvement or productive equipment."[10] The refrain is familiar. If anything, the problems of agricultural development in Ethiopia are even more complex than in colonial territories, where a planned and directed use of land can be more easily established. In regard to cotton and other large-scale agricultural output, a difficult question is the manner in which land tenure and land ownership are defined. The complexities of this subject in Ethiopia have already been described.

As might be expected, cooperative farming has failed to obtain even the slightest foothold in Ethiopia. Here is surely a device that would enable the ordinary peasant, if lack of capital were his only problem, to surmount the sometimes prohibitive cost of purchasing improved agricultural implements. But the idea of self-help through association with other farmers, with all the advantages that such cooperation entails (increased purchasing power, better marketing facilities, cheaper tools and equipment, improved farming methods), has

[10] *New Times and Ethiopia News*, May 7, 1955.

no precedent in the past to which the Ethiopian farmer is socially and mentally committed. Cooperative farming requires a mentality of an altogether different sort, a business mentality with an eye to efficiency and profit, which is simply beyond the ability of the ordinary Ethiopian peasant to grasp under present conditions. The government is seemingly apathetic about cooperative farming, possibly because it fears the possible political consequences of the idea of associations of peasants.

The principle of cooperative effort, if once grasped and carried out, could also be usefully applied to the construction of small earth-filled dams, tanks, or dugouts for the conservation of water. Water is one of the great needs of Ethiopian agriculture, for although rainfall is abundant, it is largely concentrated in only a few months of the year and quickly runs off, in the absence of catchments or storage facilities, leaving the earth parched and dry. Some irrigation is practiced in Ethiopia, where rivers make this possible, but many river beds are dry for the greater part of the year. As a result, women—the traditional heavy laborers of Ethiopia—must walk miles daily to some isolated spring or pool, with heavy clay water jugs on their backs, to provide for household needs. Cattle are often driven many miles for water (and for salt), and become thin and scrawny from lack of green forage in the long dry season. Where irrigation for crops is not available, farming is limited to what can be produced in the rainy season.

To remedy this situation farmers could band together to excavate earth tanks to impound rain water, a practice that has been adopted in many other countries, and to construct canals and troughs for irrigation and for watering cattle. At least a beginning could be made this way, with government advice and encouragement. The government's feeling seems to be that large-scale engineering schemes must be awaited.[11]

[11] As an example of the government's lethargy even when ready-made facilities are provided, one may cite the case of the numerous water wells drilled on government land by the Sinclair Petroleum Company in the Ogaden semidesert. Although water is a vital necessity and an extremely scarce one here, these wells are not being maintained and are deteriorating rapidly.

No one knows how many cattle, sheep, or goats exist in Ethiopia, just as no one knows the size of the human population. FAO estimates contained in a report to the government dated December 1954 give the following figures, which are probably as good as any: 15 million cattle (zebu), 12 million sheep, 13 million goats, 3 million horses, mules, and donkeys, and 600,000 camels. These animals are for the most part to be found all over the country, but especially large concentrations of cattle occur in the lowlands among the nomads and seminomadic tribes.

Cattle in Ethiopia, as in many primitive lands, are regarded as a sign of wealth, and in some parts of the country (as among certain primitive tribes of the south) they are even regarded as sacred and not to be eaten. Elsewhere, however, and more generally, cattle are used as food, to provide traction in plowing, and for the hides and skins they yield. Among the nomadic tribes of the southern and eastern deserts the milk from cattle and the meat they provide are almost the only source of nourishment, since agriculture is unknown to these people, and, indeed, the desolate regions in which they live could not support any.

Ethiopian cattle are all of the zebu (hump-backed) variety. They are often scrawny and underfed, and the meat is tough, owing to the length of the dry season and the lack of fodder, such as alfalfa, for their consumption. Oxen lose about fifty pounds during the dry season. The quality of the meat is poor, a great many of the animals are diseased, and the milk production is extremely low, 1½ to 2 liters per day. An FAO expert maintains that "trials for improved cattle breeding will almost certainly remain unsuccessful until feeding conditions are improved."[12]

FAO has been active, lately in cooperation with Point Four, in a program of country-wide cattle vaccination dating back to 1949. The most serious cattle disease in Ethiopia is rinderpest, from which a million and a half animals die yearly. (The diseased meat is nevertheless eaten by the Ethiopians.) The next most serious is contagious pleuro-pneumonia. Anthrax, worms, black leg, pioplasmosis, ana-

[12] FAO Report to the Government of Ethiopia on Small Agricultural Implements, No. 194 (Rome, October 1953).

plasmosis, and trypanosomniasis are less serious; they affect horses, donkeys, and mules as well as cattle. Vaccination has been given mainly for rinderpest, against which some three million cattle were treated in the first six years of the program. Although cattle vaccination is by law now compulsory, this law, like so many others, is not enforced, and some provincial governors openly oppose the program and advise the peasants not to have their livestock vaccinated. Some of the Ethiopian authorities cannot understand that cattle must be vaccinated *before* disease strikes, not after. Such are the facts as stated to the author by a former chief of the FAO mission to Ethiopia.

It is a common observation in Ethiopia that the land is overgrazed, abetting erosion, and that the cattle population of the country seems to bear little relation to the available pasture. While some likely areas have few cattle, extensive herds may be seen in semidesert country, where no grazing exists and where the cattle are reduced to obtaining food from succulent tree shoots. Little or no care is given them, and almost no provision is made to lay in a store of fodder for use in the dry season. The strain is constantly weakened because it is the practice to take the strongest bulls for plowing and leave the inferior ones for breeding. Herds of cattle are left in the care of small boys of seven or eight, and often mixed with horses, sheep, and goats. Fences are rarely encountered, and even in Addis Ababa it is not unusual to see several cows or horses wandering in the heart of the town, in the thick of the automobile traffic, heedless of and unheeded by the municipal police.

Horses are little used for plowing, if at all; they serve mainly as pack animals or for human transport. Other human and pack transport is provided by mules and donkeys. Sheep are kept for their skins, which are frequently worn as a rough, loose cloak, and for food. Goatskins are a valuable export, as are other hides and skins. Goat meat is eaten, but goat's milk is seldom drunk.

Ethiopian sheep are small and have small horns and wide, flat tails. The wool is very short and coarse, and has much kemp. It is more like the hair of a dog than true wool. The yield is very low. Very little is done to improve the breed, and as a consequence sheep produce just enough wool to keep themselves warm. The little wool that is produced is spun and woven by hand into blankets or a rough type of cloak. Some experiments have been made in and around Addis Ababa to cross-breed foreign merino sheep (first introduced into the country by the Italians) with the local variety, but success has not been very great, probably owing to the inferior conditions of forage encountered in Ethiopia. As with cattle, pasturage is inadequate, and the grasses soon lose their succulence in the dry season.

There are no statistics available on the production and consumption of meat, milk, or butter—or on the number of chickens in the country (there are a great many) or the production of eggs. A good deal of information, however, is available concerning hide and skin production, especially for the export market, and the methods used in this undertaking. Much of what follows is extracted from an FAO report on the subject.[13]

In Ethiopia the take-off of hides and skins each year is surplus to the leather requirements of the country, and beyond its tanning capacity. The total value of hide and skin exports is about Eth.$15–20 million annually; what percentage this constitutes of the total value of production is not accurately known. Exporting firms have in recent years tried to improve the preparation of hides and skins, and legislation with a similar end in view has been on the statute books for over a decade. Livestock owners and others use crude drying methods and are generally careless about branding, flaying, fleshing, cleansing, turning, folding, and marketing the product. The FAO report states that "Masks, tails, and claws are left on, and foreign matter deliberately smeared over the commodity to increase the weight. Other abuses, such as re-soaking in water, occur. Hides are book-folded; this causes cracking on opening along the lines of the folds."

Cattle hides are frequently sun-dried on the ground instead of being shade-dried on frames. As a result, hides become scratched, and dirt and other foreign matter collect on them. On the other hand, suspension drying of goatskins has already been generally adopted

[13] FAO Report to the Government of Ethiopia on Improvement, Preparation, and Processing of Hides and Skins, No. 303 (Rome, December 1954).

throughout the country, and the same practice is applied to about 70 per cent of the sheepskins marketed. The skins are better processed and handled than the hides because of the simplicity of the suspension methods employed. Also, a much greater price premium exists for properly dried skins than for hides. Horse hides are not salvaged.

There are over a hundred local markets in the country where hides and skins are traded weekly and where representatives of the hides and skins trade gather to purchase the raw hides from farmers. The present practice in these markets is one of flat price payments by the piece, irrespective of quality, type, or grade. This is clearly not conducive to creating an incentive among native producers toward improvements in quality. Green hides and skins are also sold at these trading centers, a practice which should be discouraged. Unfortunately, there is no provision in the Ministry of Agriculture's budget for hides and skins improvement work.

Slaughtering in Ethiopia is mainly a local affair; only a few of the larger towns have slaughterhouses. A Swiss-Israeli firm operates a slaughterhouse in Asmara (Eritrea) and one in Djibouti, French Somaliland, and has made efforts to obtain a similar concession at Dire Dawa. Other foreign firms have shown an interest in the construction of a series of modern slaughterhouses in the interior, but no capital has yet been committed to such an enterprise. Many problems, including cattle disease, transportation, hygiene, storage facilities, and—not least—the reluctance of some cattle owners to exchange their wealth on the hoof for cash, will first have to be overcome before this potentially lucrative field of investment can be successfully invaded.

To aid agriculture, where the problem is one of lack of capital for development, an Agricultural and Commercial Bank was founded in the capital in 1945. It had a capitalization of Eth.$1 million, and its function was primarily to extend small loans to farmers at low rates of interest. Some years later it was also permitted to extend commercial loans. The institution is now defunct, having been absorbed by the Ethiopian Development Bank, mentioned earlier. The Development Bank serves industry as well as agriculture and commerce, but on the whole its effect on the economy has not yet been appreciable. One of the main reasons for this, as should by now be apparent to the reader, is that the need it proposes to serve—the provision of adequate institutional facilities for small-scale financing—is not the most pressing in Ethiopia. While social and political conditions remain as backward as they are, a ready supply of capital alone can do little to initiate a cumulative economic advance.

VII

Trade and Commerce

Although the Ethiopian economy is virtually self-contained and provides largely for its own needs, agricultural exports are important as providing a means whereby the minimum of imports (largely textiles) that the country requires can be obtained. Since 1945, both exports and imports have been growing, and quite rapidly. The reasons for this development will shortly be discussed. Meanwhile, a brief digression.

The growth of trade and commerce in an underdeveloped country is largely reflective of the measure by which static and rudimentary consumption habits of the indigenous population can be altered and placed on a dynamic basis. In other words, it is directly reflective of the emergence among the people of new wants, desires, and dissatisfactions that have not previously existed, or of which they were at least not aware. Of course, it is a measure of ability to buy as well, which derives from the presence of income-producing assets for which a ready demand exists. But that is the other side of the coin. Given a certain basic level of agricultural production and a surplus available for exchange, the rapidity with which the demand side of this equation can be expanded is largely a question of creating new wants (in an economic sense), and then of increasing the means to pay for their satisfaction.

When the exchange economy of a country is still very small in relation to the total of what is produced, this stimulation of new wants is a slow and difficult process. In developed countries such wants are continually being stimulated by advertisement in the press and by radio and television, and appeal is made by the producers to a whole set of cultural motivations. No such conditions exist in primitive lands. The natural human desire for social recognition and prestige is there satisfied by other means. In backward countries there are practically no advertising media, and, indeed, there is little to advertise. Moreover, for most goods the size of the effective market is very small in relation to the total population.

The problem, then, is one of gradually broadening this market by creating in the population new economic, social, and cultural motivations that will lead to an increase in their consumption of manufactured goods. In underdeveloped countries there are a number of forces at work in this direction, but there are also numerous retarding influences. On the positive side one of the strongest forces is the presence among the indigenous population of foreigners with "superior" consumption habits, which they unwittingly demonstrate. These habits are first adopted by the small, relatively educated native "elite," who pass them on to their inferiors in the economic and social scale. Thus a little leaven gradually leavens the whole loaf. But the power of tradition in such countries is strong, and old ways of living and of thinking are not changed quickly. The process of education is a slow one. Thus windfall incomes, such as Ethiopia has been earning from its coffee exports in recent years, are not returned in equal measure to the market, but are hoarded. Imports lag behind exports, and consumption behind production. Although there is a surplus available for exchange, the limited scale of economic wants inhibits the growth of trade and commerce, and the extra cash goes into the ground.

Nevertheless, there has been a considerable increase in Ethiopia's foreign trade over prewar levels, and it may with fairness be asked how this has come about.

Before the war with Italy, Ethiopian foreign trade was very small, both absolutely and in relation to that of neighboring African states. Total trade has been estimated, during this period, at Eth.$20–25 million per year (exports plus imports). On the export side it seems to have consisted almost entirely of coffee, cereals, hides, skins, and beeswax, and on the import side of cheap cotton textiles. Ethiopia has never been a trading nation, landlocked and isolated as she was for much of her history. The Amharas, even today, are peculiarly averse to commerce, considering it beneath their dignity. Amhara shopkeepers are a rarity in Ethiopia, most of the retail trade being carried on by Greeks, Armenians, and Arabs.

During the Italian occupation there was a spectacular rise in imports, owing to the heavy program of construction and roadbuilding which the conquerors had undertaken in the country and the consumption requirements of the sizable new Italian settlements in Ethiopia. The rise in imports was something like 3,000 per cent. On the other hand, exports fell off to levels even lower than those prevailing before the invasion. Thus the mushroom growth of foreign trade was wholly one-sided and certainly not representative of what could have been expected to develop on a long-term basis.[1]

These distortions continued for some years after the liberation, though in far milder and in altogether different form. Allied military requirements necessitated a joint Anglo-Ethiopian administration of the country, which led to a problem of multiple currency: the British and Italian currencies both circulated in Ethiopia alongside the traditional Maria Theresa thaler.

It is only in the period following the liberation that reasonably reliable customs figures begin to appear. The whole customs apparatus was redesigned by a British adviser, and new tariffs set. The earliest figures available from this reformed administration, covering the Ethiopian year 1935 (Gregorian calendar year ending September 10, 1943) give a total for exports of £2.9 million, or Eth.$29 million in terms of the new national currency introduced in 1945. Even so, the returns are not complete, since they exclude at least Gambeila, an Ethiopian point of exit and entry near the Sudan border

---

[1] The economic effects of this immense investment (some U.S.$300–400 million went into roadbuilding alone) will be dealt with in somewhat greater detail later on. Here it is intended to speak only of the development of Ethiopian foreign trade over the past quarter century, in which the Italian occupation period played a short, though very important, part.

in the west. Total imports for the same period are recorded in the customs returns as £2.6 million, approximately. For the next Ethiopian year, ending September 10, 1944, the figures are given as 26.1 million Maria Theresa thalers each for exports and imports.[2] It is not certain whether this figure represents the value of merchandise at the Ethiopian border or at inland customs stations (all later import valuations, up to the end of 1954, include the cost of freight to inland customs points), and, in any case, imports through Gambeila are excluded. Moreover, the values are in Maria Theresa thalers, rather than in pounds, which makes for difficulty of comparison in view of the fluctuating value of the thaler during this period.

It is not until 1945 that we get the first reliable figures concerning Ethiopia's foreign trade. The data for that year (ending December 9, since this is the closest approach that can be made to a Gregorian basis by adding the appropriate quarters of two Ethiopian years) show that total exports reached Eth.$38.1 million, and imports Eth.$36.2 million. When allowance is made for internal freight, it becomes apparent that there was actually a trade surplus in that year of some Eth.$5.1 million. It is also apparent that foreign trade as a whole is already much greater—three or four times greater—than in the period before the Italian occupation. Of course, the vast Italian imports of capital and consumption goods ceased abruptly in 1941. Since then trade has continued to grow, and a decade after the end of the war the value of exports and imports was in the neighborhood of Eth.$160 million each, more than quadruple the 1945 figures and sixteen times the pre-1935 level. Nevertheless, the total value of exports still comprises less than 10 per cent of the country's gross national product.

The reasons for this large expansion of Ethiopia's foreign trade are manifold. One is that the Italian motor road system of over 4,000 miles, half of which were tarred or macadamized, opened up the country for the first time; it permitted the produce of remote provinces to be brought to market for export, and it equally facilitated the distribution of imports. Another reason is related to the crumbling

[2] The Maria Theresa thaler was officially equated at one to one with the Ethiopian dollar upon the latter's introduction in July 1945.

of the ancient semifeudal system in operation before the war and its gradual replacement by a semimodern administrative and legal structure. The cost of government was much increased, and hence import requirements were greater, if only to maintain, on a skeleton basis, the expensive Italian economic structure of roads and public services. In addition, there were many more thousands of foreigners in the country after the war than before, people whose consumption requirements had to be met and whose presence contributed greatly to raise the level of exports and commercial activity. Ethiopians' wants had themselves increased as a result of their wider contact with foreigners.[3] The introduction of an Ethiopian national currency in 1945 and the changeover to the collection of taxes in cash instead of in kind also contributed to the rise in economic activity.

In recent years, the greatest benefits to the Ethiopian economy have come from the successive jumps in the world price of coffee, Ethiopia's main export, and from the general stimulus of the Korean war. World coffee prices more than tripled between April 1949 and April 1955 (they later leveled off to approximately double the early 1949 level). In Ethiopia, owing to the progressively heavier export tax on coffee as the world price rises, the maximum fluctuations have not been quite as extreme as on the world market, but otherwise the price trends have been parallel. Naturally, combined with a substantial increase in Ethiopian production, from an average annual export of some 15,500 metric tons before 1949 to approximately 42,000 tons in 1955, these sharp coffee price rises served to increase greatly the total value of Ethiopia's exports.[4]

Other exports have also increased, in volume and in value, since the end of the war, although no other Ethiopian export approaches the importance of coffee. Over 80 per cent of the total value of Ethi-

[3] The Italian occupation itself had a considerable influence in this respect. Referring to this aspect of the occupation, one Ethiopian of some education confided to the writer that he considered the Italian episode "the best thing that has ever happened to the country."

[4] A further statistical increase of at least 10 per cent has been recorded in Ethiopian exports since 1952 as the result of political federation with Eritrea.

opian exports consists of just a few major agricultural commodity groups: coffee, hides and skins, cereals, pulses, and oilseeds. Oilseeds were of only minor importance in 1945; ten years later they ranked second, next to coffee, accounting for 11 per cent of the total value of all exports in 1955. The export of wheat flour, on the other hand, which is manufactured mainly by several Greek-owned mills in Addis Ababa, has decreased just as phenomenally, and it is of negligible importance today. In 1955 the chief items in Ethiopia's export economy were the following: coffee, 56 per cent; oilseeds, 11 per cent; hides and skins, 10 per cent; cereals and pulses, 6 per cent. Beeswax, which had some importance before 1935, is exported in negligible amounts today. With the exception of khat—a highly stimulating plant consumed in certain parts of the Middle East—the balance of Ethiopian exports is chiefly made up of small quantities of a miscellaneous assortment of agricultural and manufactured items, the latter mainly from Eritrea, such as civet, honey, ghee, fresh vegetables, cement, mother-of-pearl buttons, fish meal, frozen and canned meat, beer, and salt. The export of live cattle, which reached sizable proportions for the first time in 1955, is likely to be of growing importance. Cattle are exported at present largely by a Swiss-Israeli firm with slaughterhouse, canning, and freezing facilities at Asmara and Djibouti. (The animals are carefully quarantined and observed to control disease.)

One of the interesting developments in Ethiopia's foreign trade has been the relative decline in the importance of certain items, such as textiles, and the corresponding increase in the importance of capital goods imports. Thus, whereas textiles before the war accounted for over four-fifths of the country's total imports, by 1950 the proportion had dropped to approximately half and in 1955 it was just under one-third. Along with the over-all expansion of trade, and the considerable increase in diversification, there has been an expansion of imports satisfying in the main industrial, construction, and transportation needs. Items of this nature have increased in relative importance from roughly 10 per cent of total imports in 1945 to well over 35 per cent of total imports after 1956.

In 1955 the main purchasers of Ethiopian exports were the United

States, Italy, the United Kingdom, Saudi Arabia, and Germany. Ethiopia's main suppliers were Italy, the United States, India, the United Kingdom, Japan, Germany, and France; these seven countries furnished a little over three-fourths of Ethiopia's total import requirements. The corresponding export percentages cannot be determined exactly, because a large part of exports listed in the Ethiopian trade returns as destined for Aden and Djibouti are in reality transshipped elsewhere, most of them to the United States. (United States figures for imports from Ethiopia are more than twice as great as Ethiopian figures for exports to the United States.)

Some 90 per cent of Ethiopian exports to the United States are coffee. It may thus be deduced with some accuracy that the United States is far and away Ethiopia's best customer, taking annually around 50 per cent of her exports and approximately 75 per cent of her coffee. Another observation of some significance is that Italy has managed to retain a strong foothold in Ethiopia's economy, being her leading supplier (about 15 per cent of total) and her second largest buyer (about 17 per cent of total). Russia and the Iron Curtain countries have practically no place in Ethiopian foreign trade.

The commerce of the country is largely in the hands of a multitude of small Armenian, Indian, Greek, and Arab merchants. The Ethiopians themselves have shown no aptitude for trade and have, in fact, traditionally evinced a strong dislike for it. On the wholesale level there are a number of large foreign firms with considerable invested capital operating in Addis Ababa and other principal centers. Unfortunately, no data are available on the total investment of foreign, or even of domestic, capital in commercial undertakings, since there is no law requiring companies to keep accounting records or to furnish statistical information. Most firms, in fact, are extremely reluctant to disclose any details of their financial operations, fearing higher taxes, and some do not even keep proper books. Nevertheless, some estimate, however rough, can be made of this total, based on the known number of firms in the field and their estimated average size. The Ministry of Commerce's handbook of 1955 entitled *Economic Progress of Ethiopia* lists 105 exporters and importers in Ethiopia and approximately the same number in Eritrea. A footnote to the Eritrean list states that only firms with a declared capital of Eth.$35,000 or over are included. In addition, there are a number of firms engaged in retail trade only that are not included in the total. It is probably not far wide of the mark to state that the number of trading firms, not including manufacturing and industrial establishments, in the Ethiopian Empire is between 200 and 250. The total investment in these commercial enterprises is presumably between Eth.-$50 million and Eth.$75 million. Perhaps another Eth.$75 million to Eth.$100 million is invested in industrial establishments (excluding public utilities) in Ethiopia and Eritrea, which number about 300.

The commerce of the country is largely concerned with the purchase of agricultural commodities from primary producers for export, and with the distribution of imports. The internal economy is for the most part self-sustaining and self-sufficient, with little exchange of goods and hence with little need for money. Indeed, barter is still carried on in many parts of the country. Paper currency notes are accepted in most areas, but almost everywhere coins, especially silver coins, are much preferred.

There are no figures available on the numbers of Ethiopians employed in commerce, but the total is certainly not large, probably not in excess of 20,000, including Eritrea. For manufacturing the total may approximate 25,000 or 30,000, again including Eritrea. The number of Ethiopians in commerce and manufacturing together comes to no more than one-half of 1 per cent of the country's population. Undoubtedly the largest employer of Ethiopians outside of agriculture, industry, and commerce is the government. The servant class is also very large; wages are so low that even servants maintain servants. Other Ethiopians are employed in the transportation field, or in the construction industry as day laborers. There are also a considerable number of idlers, although few outright beggars, since the strong sense of family ties and the surplus agricultural output in Ethiopia rule out any serious chance of starvation. In some instances these same factors place a premium on idleness and prevent the industrious from accumulating even small savings—a host of near and distant relatives will see to that.

There is no Sears Roebuck in Ethiopia to which the country people can apply for merchandise by mail. The larger towns have retail outlets, but most of them are rather crude affairs and their proprietors are unacquainted with the most elementary advertising or public relations techniques. Only in Addis Ababa and Asmara are occasional retail distribution facilities met with that approximate a European or American standard. For the most part, the distribution of imported goods in the interior of the country is carried on by itinerant Greek or Arab traders, who buy their supplies from the towns and then transport them by mule to different local markets, to which people flock from miles around on designated market days. Agents of some of the larger export-import firms may also be present to barter textiles and other goods against the purchase of coffee, hides, or grain from native growers. Haggling is common, indeed the expected practice. Going to market is a social event of prime importance, as well as an economic one, and offers an opportunity—almost the only one in the life of the ordinary peasant—to meet with people from distant areas and to exchange gossip and news. It is beyond dispute that more and better roads, especially small feeder roads, would do more than almost anything else to open up the country and thus stimulate commerce by permitting the establishment of a greater number of permanent trading posts or shops to which people would find it easier to go for their purchases.

VIII

Banking and Currency

The monetary side of Ethiopia's economy, although small in relation to the total value of output, has nevertheless for some time required the use of certain banking facilities, especially for the proper conduct of foreign trade. Such facilities have existed for a little over half a century. The first Ethiopian bank, the Bank of Abyssinia, was established in 1905 under control of the National Bank of Egypt. Business was very slow—in fact, operations were conducted at a loss—until the completion of the railway to Addis Ababa in 1917, when conditions gradually began to improve. In 1931 the Bank of Abyssinia was bought out from Egyptian control by the Emperor Haile Selassie, and a purely Ethiopian institution, the Bank of Ethiopia, was established in its place. It was short-lived, its activities being brought to a close by the Italians in 1935–36. During the occupation the Italians set up their own banks, branches of the Banco di Roma, but these, in turn, were forced to close upon the defeat of the Italian forces by British and patriot troops in 1941. The most urgent and immediate banking requirements were then met for a time by the establishment of a branch of Barclay's Bank (D. C. & O.) in the capital. The restored Ethiopian government, however, wanted an Ethiopian bank and in 1942 replaced Barclay's Bank with a new institution, the State Bank of Ethiopia.

The State Bank of Ethiopia is a corporate entity. It was established by imperial proclamation on August 26, 1942, but it did not come into operation until the following year. The original capital investment, fully subscribed by the Ministry of Finance, amounted to one million Maria Theresa thalers, the currency then in force along with the East African shilling. The charter of the State Bank was published in November 1943 — nearly eight months after the bank had opened for business — and outlined in detail the powers and functions of the new institution. Final control of the bank's affairs was vested in the hands of the government, although active direction of its day-to-day operations was placed in the hands of a governor and subordinate officers, presided over by an Ethiopian board of directors. The State Bank became the central bank of the Empire, being empowered to issue banknotes and coins as agent of the Ministry of Finance, and upon the subsequent withdrawal of Barclay's Bank it also became the sole bank in the country to engage in normal commercial banking transactions. A branch of the Banque de l'Indo-Chine was opened in February 1943, but it does not normally accept deposits and it is not permitted to engage in the sale or purchase of foreign exchange. Since Ethiopian-Eritrean federation several branches of Italian banks previously operating in Eritrea have been allowed to continue in business, but their activities have been greatly curtailed as a result of the State Bank's monopoly of foreign exchange operations. In recent years it has been announced that foreign banking competition will shortly be welcomed in Ethiopia, although under what terms and conditions is not yet plain, as the long-pending banking law of the country has not yet been promulgated.

The State Bank of Ethiopia began operations in April 1943 under a Canadian governor, Mr. C. S. Collier. Since then it has had a number of foreign (mostly American) governors, under whose direction the State Bank of Ethiopia has become one of the most successful financial institutions in Ethiopia. It may be remarked with some truth, however, that its monopoly position in the field might have assured it of success in any event.

When the bank first began operations, business was conducted on a rather small scale, the number of employees totaling only about fifteen (in 1956 this number had risen to over 600). Services offered included current accounts, issuance of drafts, mail, and telegraphic transfers, letters of credit, foreign exchange, and loans against mortgages, merchandise, and personal guarantee. Overdraft facilities were also extended to a few firms. The bank's early years were marked by fairly rapid growth, reflecting a concomitant expansion in all phases of economic activity, both government and private. The bank showed a loss for the year 1943, owing largely to costs involved in starting operations and opening branches, but since then it has earned a profit in each fiscal period.

Correspondent accounts were opened with numerous banks abroad. The State Bank currently maintains about three dozen such accounts in some eighteen countries of the world. An Issue Department was added to the bank in July 1945, by virtue of the Currency and Legal Tender Proclamation of that year, and customer services and the number of branches were gradually increased. Savings facilities were made available to the public by the head office in January 1946, and since then have been extended to most branches.

The extension of banking facilities into the various provinces of the Empire has been a significant development in Ethiopian banking. Some of the branches are not commercially profitable, but they have been maintained in these remote areas so that the people may become acquainted with Ethiopian currency and banking facilities. The branches provide all banking services, but must refer requests for foreign exchange to Addis Ababa—a time-consuming procedure.[1] Loan activity is low in most branches, and a number of them do not have more than a bookkeeper, a manager, and a large sum of cash, plus a few current accounts. Ten of the sixteen branches operated at a loss in 1954 and 1955, and about the same number in 1956 and 1957. Nevertheless, the branches considered as a whole have produced a thumping profit in recent years as a result of the highly profitable operations of the Asmara and Dire Dawa offices.

The amount of cash held in the branches is extraordinary, in relation both to their size and to what is held at the head office. With the exception of the largest branches (Asmara and Dire Dawa), branch holdings of cash represent in most cases well over 90 per cent—some-

[1] The Eritrean branches (except Assab) are under the control of the Asmara office.

times up to 99 per cent—of assets, compared with less than 25 per cent for the head office. With an extremely low level of provincial borrowing from banks and small deposits on the part of the public, it may be asked why such huge cash holdings are necessary, or how they arise. The answer is simple: there is no checking system to speak of, no popularly accepted way to transfer the ownership of money without transporting physical cash. Outside of a few major towns payment by check is virtually unknown in Ethiopia. Even certified checks of the State Bank have been refused by the customs authorities at Assab and Massawa. Hence, merchants doing business in the interior are required to pay and collect for purchases and sales in cash, with metallic currency preferred.

According to the season and the rhythm of the market, cash flows into rural branch banks as merchants deposit sales proceeds for transfer to the capital or elsewhere, and flows out again as transfers are made in the opposite direction to pay for the purchase of agricultural produce. Payment in cash is required, since native growers have, for the most part, no accounts with the local bank. The whole process is very cumbersome; an enormous amount of time and effort is spent in counting currency notes and coins and transporting them back and forth. Even at Addis Ababa payment by check is the exception rather than the rule, and it is common practice for merchants to arrive at the bank each morning with suitcases full of one-dollar notes for counting and deposit.

With the steady addition of new branches and the expansion of facilities and accounts at head office, the position of the State Bank in the economic life of the country has become increasingly important. The bank has grown with the needs of trade and has earned a reputation for financial soundness and conservative banking practice. Its profit reached Eth.$3.1 million in 1955 (compared to only a few hundred thousand dollars in 1944, its first full year of operations), and its total assets more than quadrupled in the decade 1945–55. Deposits in the same period grew from Eth.$12.7 million to Eth.$112.8 million. Government deposits constituted somewhat less than 60 per cent of the 1955 total; amounts held in savings and time deposit accounts made up some 13 per cent. Loans and advances have also increased over the years, but here the factor of growth has been much less impressive. In part this is a reflection of the relative scarcity of local investment opportunities, but it is also due to the bank's highly conservative loan policy. For example, it has been the practice to extend mortgage loans for very short periods only, at high rates of interest, and even today the maximum maturity of such loans is a mere four years.[2] This must discourage many small builders from borrowing. Despite the high rate of defaults among Ethiopian borrowers, a more liberal loan policy would seem to be desirable, both from the point of view of stimulating economic growth and from that of more fully utilizing the bank's earning assets.

Approximately 8 per cent of the Eth.$15.8 million of outstanding loans and advances at the end of 1955 had been made to the government, which is exempt from the payment of interest. In earlier years, government loans accounted for a very large part of the total, but there has been a definite tendency away from direct government borrowing from the bank. Theoretically, such direct borrowing has been limited by law since 1950 to a total of Eth.$3 million. In addition to permissible "indirect" borrowing of Eth.$2 million, however, the government still may legally obtain funds from the bank through the "sale" of its promissory notes, termed Treasury Bills, as described in Chapter V. Up to the end of 1955 some Eth.$62 million had been so "borrowed," interest-free and with no obligation of redemption, and another Eth.$25 million was taken in March 1956, thus sharply cutting into the excess reserves of the Issue Department. These stood at 36.8 per cent of the currency fund reserve at the end of March 1956, not much above the 30 per cent minimum required by law. Thus the government took from the bank, to supplement its revenue from other sources, a total of nearly Eth.$78 million in the six years prior to April 1956, out of a total of Eth.$110 million in foreign exchange accumulated during the same period as the result of successive balance-of-payments surpluses. Most of this went to swell the total of govern-

[2] For the first time since its inception the State Bank reduced all loan interest rates by one percentage point as of November 15, 1955. These now range from 6 to 8 per cent depending on the type of loan, with mortgage loans at 7 per cent.

ment deposits with the State Bank; very little was invested in capital projects. As a consequence, the inflationary effect of this sizable increment in the money supply (which stood at some Eth.$241 million as of December 31, 1955) has been negligible. In view of the fact that these funds have been left largely idle, with the government's cash position at the State Bank very satisfactory, it is difficult to understand the purpose behind the borrowing of an additional Eth.$25 million in March 1956.

Total earnings of the State Bank were larger in 1955 than in any previous year. Its net profit that year was below the 1954 peak, however, owing to the setting up in 1955 of a large provision for bad and doubtful debts that had not been carried as an expense item before. Income from foreign exchange transactions constituted the bank's major source of earnings (53 per cent of the total), as in other years. Interest and discount earned on loans and advances, as well as on foreign investments, accounted for 35 per cent of total earnings; commissions and other income accounted for 12 per cent. Roughly half of the total interest earned by the bank derives from its foreign investments, which are mostly in long-term U.S. dollar bonds of the IBRD.

As a result of the balance-of-payments surplus which Ethiopia again enjoyed in 1955 (Eth.$14.3 million compared to Eth.$22.7 million in 1954 and a peak of Eth.$44.9 million in 1953), foreign monetary reserves of the central bank reached a new year-end high of Eth.$151.4 million on December 31, 1955, 9 per cent above the corresponding 1954 figure of Eth.$139.1 million. The proportion of U.S. dollar holdings at the end of 1955 rose to 87 per cent of the combined reserves of foreign securities and foreign balances, compared to 82½ per cent a year before and to less than 20 per cent in 1950. If gold reserves are added, the proportion is even higher. At the end of 1955 the State Bank's capital had grown to sixteen times the original investment.

There is no doubt of the strong financial position the State Bank has attained, particularly over the last six years as the result of heavy coffee exports. By the same token, however, a serious drop in coffee prices could mean trouble; and coffee may someday be a glut on the market, owing to the heavy plantings in all countries that followed the sharp successive price increases dating approximately from 1949. This is just one more argument for greater crop diversification and a substantial improvement in quality.

In brief, the State Bank's success since its inception in 1943 has been notable, but not entirely due to its own efforts. The fortunes of the export market have been decisive, and the lack of competition in the banking field has been helpful. The untrained and inexperienced Ethiopian board of directors has contributed little, although some observers have remarked that the bank's standard of operations is superior to that of comparable banks in other Middle Eastern countries. The bank's largely Ethiopian staff is ill-trained and inefficient, many of its methods are obsolete, and its quarters are overcrowded. The bank suffers, in addition, from a seemingly unavoidable but deadly nepotism that is the lot of nearly all government, and of some private, operations in Ethiopia; from a lack of continuity in policy; and from a regrettable lack of firmness in decision and execution. It is, however, absolutely sound financially, and strong in the matter of its foreign reserves. If its policies have been overconservative, they at least have had the virtue of protecting it from dangerous fiscal ventures and have thus helped to establish it in a position of respect and authority in the eyes of both the foreign and the domestic business community.

Although some form of money had been in use in Ethiopia during earlier times, the present fairly widespread acceptance of a paper currency is of recent origin. Most of the internal trade of the country was for long carried on by means of barter, employing blocks of salt, lengths of cloth, and iron. About the middle of the nineteenth century the large silver coin known as the Maria Theresa thaler, first minted in Austria in 1751, came into circulation, and it remained the coin most generally accepted throughout the country until the currency reform of 1945. (Even today these ancient coins circulate in a few remote parts of Ethiopia, and certain taxes are received in them, although they have long been outlawed.) The Maria Theresa thaler was esteemed not only for its intrinsic worth—it was $83\frac{1}{3}$ per cent silver—but for its decorative and easily recognizable design as well.

About fifty million of these coins are estimated to have been in circulation on the eve of the Italian invasion of 1935.

Neither the issuance of an Ethiopian metal coinage under Menelik II and Haile Selassie nor the printing of some notes by the Bank of Ethiopia prior to 1935 met with any appreciable success in replacing the silver thalers. During the occupation the Italians attempted to introduce their own currency, the lira, but were at last compelled—to prevent the complete stagnation of trade—to reintroduce the Maria Theresa thaler. (They had purchased the master dies from Vienna in 1932.)[3]

With the Italian defeat in 1941 the currency situation became more confused than ever, since the British troops that liberated the country brought with them a large quantity of East African shillings. A third currency was thus added to the two others in circulation, the lira and the Maria Theresa thaler, and all three were declared legal tender.

The difficulties of the restored Ethiopian government were increased by the limitations placed on its control of the currency by the Anglo-Ethiopian Agreement of 1942. A second agreement, in December 1944, however, removed these restrictions and opened the way for the establishment of a new, and purely Ethiopian, currency. The necessity for some such action was becoming increasingly apparent with the disruption of trade and the substantial fluctuations in the value of the several currencies in terms of each other. In addition, there existed a strong tendency to hoard Maria Theresa thalers and to ship them out of the country in view of the rising price of silver on world markets. By the end of 1944 the Maria Theresa thaler was worth three East African shillings on the free market, although it had been legally pegged at only two shillings in 1943.

The American governor of the State Bank, Mr. George Blowers, in consultation with the Ethiopian Minister of Finance, worked out the details of a new currency to be issued with the help of a large silver

---

[3] It should, perhaps, be mentioned that most of the M.T. thalers still in circulation in Ethiopia and other parts of the Middle East do not date from the original issue but are the product of more recent mintings in Western countries.

loan under lend-lease arrangement with the United States. The new currency was first issued on July 23, 1945, the Emperor's fifty-third birthday. The details of the currency reform had been published the previous May in *Negarit Gazeta* under the title of Currency and Legal Tender Proclamation, No. 76 of 1945. The new law established the Ethiopian dollar, equal in value to 5.52 grains of fine gold, as the single monetary unit of the country. The dollar is based on the decimal system and is fixed at 40.25 United States cents. The sole right of issue is vested in the Issue Department of the State Bank of Ethiopia, acting on behalf of the Ministry of Finance. As backing, the State Bank of Ethiopia maintains a currency fund consisting of gold, silver, and foreign assets (foreign bank balances or readily convertible prime securities), plus domestic obligations of the Imperial Ethiopian Government (Treasury Bills).

The original law limited the maximum proportion of Treasury Bills to 25 per cent of the currency fund and the minimum proportion of foreign assets to 75 per cent. In an amendment of 1950 the required minimum foreign coverage was reduced from 75 per cent to 30 per cent of the note issue, and the maximum proportion of Treasury Bills was correspondingly raised. As already indicated, the latter are themselves theoretically secured by a pledge of fixed assets of the Ethiopian Treasury equal to 110 per cent of these obligations. In fact, however, no such pledge exists and no specific assets are anywhere pledged. The reduction in the foreign proportion of the note issue was undertaken in order to liberate a large amount of foreign exchange badly needed in the support of imports, especially since the bank's foreign reserves had suffered a blow through the British sterling devaluation of the preceding year. The reduction was well advised, however, in view of the stability of the Ethiopian dollar and the confidence that had been shown in it since its introduction five years before. The action released a total of Eth.$17.2 million in foreign exchange for use in the support of imports and permitted a greater degree of flexibility in the money supply to meet the seasonal needs of the country's foreign trade.

After the introduction of the new currency in July 1945, East African shillings continued as legal tender for another six months, but

Maria Theresa thalers were immediately demonetized and called in for redemption by the State Bank. The demonetized thalers were treated as silver bullion, and now constitute a part of the legal backing for Ethiopian currency notes. The East African shillings in circulation at the time of the currency reform were gradually redeemed by the State Bank at the rate of two shillings per dollar. Almost 60 per cent of the original currency reserve arose from the redemption of these notes for sterling balances in London, which were later invested in gilt-edge British Empire securities. (Today, as mentioned earlier, the investment is almost entirely in U.S. dollar bonds, chiefly IBRD.) The remaining 40 per cent of the original reserve came from the normal accumulation of foreign exchange balances of the State Bank of Ethiopia, acquired through merchandise exports and the sale of newly mined gold abroad.

The note fund reserve at the end of a little less than 18 months of operations under the new currency (December 31, 1946) covered a total issue of Eth.$39.9 million in notes, composed as follows: foreign securities, 84 per cent; foreign balances, 9 per cent; silver bullion in the form of Maria Theresa thalers, 5 per cent; and Ethiopian Treasury Bills, 2 per cent. By December 31, 1955, the total issue of notes had grown to Eth.$126.4 million, composed as follows: foreign securities, 5 per cent; foreign balances, 26 per cent; silver bullion, 12 per cent; gold, 8 per cent; and Ethiopian Treasury Bills, 49 per cent. Thus, at the end of 1955 there was a backing of 51 per cent in foreign assets for the note issue, compared to the 30 per cent minimum required by law.[4] The coin issue has grown from Eth.$14.5 million to Eth.$35.8 million in the same period. In addition, gross bank deposits have expanded by Eth.$76.2 million, so that the total money supply—cash in circulation plus gross deposits[5]—approximated Eth.$241.4 million at the end of 1955, compared to Eth.$79.3 million at the end of 1946.

There is no doubt that the 1945 currency reform has enjoyed a notable, and for many a wholly unexpected, success. The currency system thus set up provided a much-needed element of elasticity in the money supply. Previously there had always been a severe shortage

[4] But see p. 102.
[5] Including government deposits.

of cash at certain times of the year, coinciding with the movement of crops to market. With the issuance of the new currency tied to the needs of trade through fluctuations in the balance of payments, this difficulty was alleviated. The traditional hold of the Maria Theresa thaler on the country's economic life has been broken, and a wide measure of confidence now exists in the national currency.

The large expansion of the money supply has kept pace, more or less, with the needs of trade and has not been inflationary. In fact, the general level of imported goods prices is much lower today than it was when records first became available in 1947. This does not, of course, tell the whole story; the prices of some locally produced and consumed commodities rose in the postwar decade, and urban rents, particularly in the capital, approximately doubled in level during the period 1950–56. The prices of meats, eggs, and vegetables in urban centers have increased substantially in recent years. There are no reliable cost-of-living figures. One of the difficulties of measuring changes in the cost of living at various urban centers in Ethiopia arises from the existence, side by side, of heterogeneous income groups (Americans, Europeans, Asiatics, and natives) having different consumption patterns that cannot easily be reflected in a single index.

For all domestic transactions, except those relating to exports and imports, regular and consistent price quotations are simply not available. In the rural areas monetary transactions are still the exception instead of the rule; the rule is barter. Regular price records are available only for Addis Ababa and Asmara, and are limited to internationally traded commodities. These records have been kept by the Statistics Department of the State Bank, and by one or two other agencies, for a number of postwar years.[6] The State Bank's indexes of export and import prices are based on transactions at the wholesale level (in the case of exports, they measure the wholesale selling prices of primary producers) and are fairly representative, being gathered weekly from over a dozen different sources covering over 90 per cent of exports and approximately 75 per cent of imports. Representative weights are used in computing group and general indexes, based on

[6] The State Bank has recently sought to collect price data for a number of other trading centers.

the relative value distribution of different items in the total of export or import trade, as the case may be, during a five-year base period.

Both the export and the import price indexes are based on the average level of prices prevailing in 1951. This appears now to have been the peak year for export prices since the war, as well as a turning point in the trend of import prices. The latter, however, had been much higher in 1947, the earliest year for which import price data are available. Export prices are in some cases available back to the beginning of 1945.

Since the monetary part of Ethiopia's economy is based so largely on foreign trade, it is to be expected that the general trend of both export and import prices reflects closely the price movements of the same commodities on world markets. These movements, as expressed in the terms of trade, have been decidedly to Ethiopia's advantage during most of the postwar period, the terms of trade rising from 61.8 in 1947 (1951 = 100) to 118.7 in 1954. They dropped to 96.2 in 1955, rose to 111.7 in 1956, and later leveled off at around 100. These favorable developments have been the result of a steady long-term reduction in the cost of Ethiopian imports (mainly textiles) in conjunction with a sharp rise in the price of the country's chief export, coffee. The future trend will depend largely on price developments in the coffee market. Export prices, on the whole, rose from the beginning of 1945 to the end of 1947, and then declined through most of 1949. The outbreak of the Korean war in June 1950 gave a renewed stimulus to commodity prices and lifted them to a post-World War II peak a year later. Since then, reflecting the gradual subsidence and eventual disappearance of war-scare buying and inventory accumulation, world commodity prices have in general been on the decline.

On the import side, Ethiopian wholesale prices have descended some distance from their apparently abnormally high levels in 1947. They, too, responded to the stimulus of Korea, reaching a peak in November 1951. By 1956 they had declined an average of 30 per cent from that peak.

Although it is difficult to isolate the influence of the world-wide currency devaluations of September 1949, they do not seem to have produced a measurable effect on the trend of Ethiopian wholesale prices. Since Ethiopia was not among the devaluing nations, the immediate effect of her refusal to devalue was an appreciation of her currency in terms of the currencies of those countries which had devalued. With the prices of her goods determined in world markets, Ethiopian exporters received less in terms of Ethiopian dollars for their produce, but this was offset by a rise in the sterling price of these goods under the stimulus of increased demand from the United States and other countries which had not devalued. The net result was that the general level of export prices remained much the same after as before devaluation, until the start of hostilities in Korea nine months later. On the import side, the devaluations appear to have slightly accelerated the downtrend in prices that had been in evidence—with one minor interruption—since quotations first became available in June 1947.

Data for the third quarter of 1957 placed the general export index for Addis Ababa at 76.1 (1951 = 100) and the general import index at 77.6 (1951 = 100). Import goods have been remarkably steady over the last several years. The general export index, on the other hand, has fluctuated considerably with the ups and downs of the coffee market. Price trends in other commodities were mixed during 1953–55, with oilseeds generally rising, hides and pulses declining, and the rest fairly stable, although with considerable seasonable fluctuations. The prices of major import commodities all showed steady to slightly declining trends over the same period, although tire prices rose about $7\frac{1}{2}$ per cent in 1955. Paper and paper products, after dropping sharply in the first half of 1955, rose just as sharply in the second half, but later declined below the level of 1953 and 1954.

A weak form of price control is legally in effect in Ethiopia, based on maximum permissible mark-ups over cost. From time to time lists of maximum permissible retail prices for individual lots of goods recently imported are published by the Ministry of Commerce and Industry. Enforcement is generally left up to the public, through the medium of complaints to official channels, since there are only a handful of government inspectors. In any event, the attempted control is limited to Addis Ababa and does not affect the rest of the country. Actually, there has been no real need for price controls: competition among retailers has been adequate, to judge from the steady decline in prices of imported goods. Occasionally an unscrupulous merchant takes advantage of a temporary shortage to jack up prices, and the public complains; but few cases of this sort have come up for trial. The public is, in any event, apathetic and largely ignorant of the existence of any form of price control.

Ethiopia is among the numerous countries of the world that practice exchange control. The establishment of an effective system of exchange control came about in September 1949, just before the world-wide currency devaluations. Legally, some form of control had existed since October 1942, and this was somewhat strengthened by an amendment of June 1948 to the Currency Proclamation of 1942. However, no regulations, methods, or procedures of control had been set up, foreign traders were largely uninformed of the law, and its application and enforcement, consequently, remained pretty much in abeyance. By Legal Notice No. 127 of 1949 this situation was altered. Detailed instructions were laid down on the mechanics of control, the State Bank of Ethiopia was declared the sole authorized dealer in foreign exchange, and in accordance with this provision an exchange control office was set up in the bank. The introduction of exchange control was considered necessary in order to strengthen the U.S. dollar position, to limit the use of foreign exchange for "nonessential" imports, and to prevent capital flights.

Ethiopia's exchange control is characterized by exchange licensing for all payments, surrender of all foreign exchange receipts, and prescription of currencies for exchange payments and receipts. There has been a great liberalization of all restrictions since the end of 1953, in view of the plenitude of exchange, and almost all requests for foreign exchange are now freely granted. Some restrictions, however, remain. These are on invisibles and on capital transactions, where limits are set according to the individual income position of the applicant. The tendency, however, is to be very liberal. In cases in which the applicant has a special contract, entitling him to remit more, exceptions are observed.

All transactions in foreign exchange must be effected through the

State Bank of Ethiopia; all payments abroad and exports are subject to the supervision of the exchange controller, whose office is a department of the State Bank. Payments outside Ethiopia must be effected in foreign exchange appropriate to the country of the recipient, and foreign exchange from exports must be surrendered in the appropriate currency, usually that of the country of final destination. In the case of coffee, surrender of exchange must be at least 50 per cent in U.S. dollars, unless it can be proved that the final destination of the coffee is a nondollar area, in which case payment in the currency of the country of final destination or in transferable sterling is accepted.

There are no import licenses, but all imports require exchange licenses (or *franco valuto* certification). As indicated, such exchange is freely granted for all goods in the appropriate currency of the country of their origin, or in a softer currency when ordered through a third country. Payment may be by cash-against-documents, mail transfer, or telegraphic transfer, but letter of credit is preferred.

Payments for invisibles also require exchange licenses. Licenses for invisibles connected with trade transactions are allowed on the same basis as the goods to which they relate. Persons traveling abroad are granted foreign exchange in the currency of the country of destination on a case-to-case basis. They may take with them a maximum of Eth.$150 in Ethiopian banknotes. Exchange for education is granted within reasonable limits in each case. Exchange for such purposes as charity and maintenance is granted in moderate amounts to residents not permanently domiciled in Ethiopia for remittances to their own country. The transfer of reasonable amounts of dividends and similar payments due to nonresidents is permitted in the currency of the original investment. Family maintenance remittances may range from Eth.$105 to Eth.$245 a month, depending on the annual income of the applicant. Special contract employees may remit more. When permanently leaving Ethiopia, an applicant may transfer abroad his assets to the extent of £10,000 a year.

In applying for an export license an exporter must indicate the amount of foreign exchange he expects to receive. Minimum requirements are established for all exports. However, the exporter remains liable for the full sales price of the proceeds. The granting of an exchange license by the exchange controller enables the goods to pass through the customs. The licensing system is used to ensure that foreign exchange receipts are surrendered to the State Bank of Ethiopia and that export proceeds are received in appropriate exchange. In due time exporters must surrender at the official rate the promised amount of currency. The exporter must also produce a certified sales certificate so that it may be verified whether he has, in fact, surrendered the total sales proceeds.

In the case of imports, there is close cooperation between the bank's Import Control Department and the Ethiopian customs to see to it that no goods are imported which do not have either an exchange license or a *franco valuto* statement to support them, and that the customs and exchange control valuations coincide.

Exchange receipts from invisibles must also be surrendered. Persons may bring into Ethiopia a maximum of Eth.$150 in Ethiopian banknotes. All foreign exchange must be declared by travelers on entry, and its subsequent use or reexport is subject to license.

All foreign exchange receipts in the form of capital must be surrendered. There is no discrimination regarding the currencies in which foreign investments are accepted. All payments abroad on account of capital are subject to individual exchange licenses. Foreign exchange is granted for repayment abroad of matured capital obligations of temporary residents. Other types of capital transfer are handled on a case-to-case basis.

Aside from the exchange control system as described above, there are no direct controls on trade, and in particular no import quotas.

Ethiopia's exchange controls, as controls, have enjoyed a fair amount of success and have succeeded in building up large official reserves of U.S. dollars. Unfortunately, optimum use has not been made of these reserves, and (as we have seen) there has been virtually no application of them to public capital development. The country has relied instead mainly on foreign loans, in recent years to a large extent on loans from the International Bank. If it seems odd that money should be borrowed at 4 and 5 per cent which could have been obtained much more cheaply and with less difficulty from the sizable foreign reserves of the central bank, it should be remembered that when the IBRD loans were contracted in 1950–51, foreign reserves were still small. After six years of mounting reserves, however, resulting in a cumulative balance-of-payments surplus since the beginning of 1950 of some Eth.$110 million, it is hard indeed to see why the government should have sought additional large loans from the International Bank and from the Export-Import Bank of Washington. A considerable part—even the entire amount—of these loans, amounting in the aggregate to U.S.$39 million, could have been financed at a substantial saving in interest out of the large foreign reserves of the State Bank. If the beneficial results of exchange control are to be voluntarily relinquished in this blunt manner, one wonders how much strength remains in the standard argument for such controls as a method of accumulating foreign capital for economic development.

Since the almost complete relaxation of exchange restrictions at the end of 1953, the State Bank's exchange control office has been exercising a largely supervisory and licensing function. As the system remains one based on individual allocations of exchange, a certain arbitrariness is unavoidable, despite the recent liberalization, in regard to what is allowed for travel abroad or for family remittance. This varies with the nationality and contractual status of the applicant, and is furthermore limited in absolute amount, in most cases. Capital transfers are also regulated, so that a person seeking to liquidate his holdings in Ethiopia may do so only gradually, within the limits of an acceptable amortization schedule. These remaining restrictions are annoying, as is the red tape and delay involved in applying for an exchange license. But they have become such an accepted part of the regulation of economic activity by governments throughout the world that their justification is seldom challenged any longer on theoretical grounds.

IX

Industry and Development

The level of industrial development in Ethiopia and Eritrea is very low; it is limited to a few hundred small-scale enterprises engaged in food processing, textile production, shoe manufacture, cement production, cigarette output, alcohol manufacture, construction and lumbering, mining and quarrying, button manufacture, match production, furniture production, soap manufacture, electric power production, and a few other miscellaneous undertakings. In Ethiopia there are also several score coffee- and grain-cleaning establishments. The total capital investment in Ethiopia and Eritrea in industry of all kinds, excluding public services, is probably between Eth.$75 million and Eth.$100 million, or no more than 5 per cent of the estimated annual gross national product of Eth.$2 billion. The largest industrial investment is one of recent origin, a sugar plantation and factory of the Dutch Handelsvereeniging (Amsterdam), some sixty miles southeast of the capital. The Dutch have invested over Eth.$20 million in this enterprise and are planning further expansion toward an eventual annual capacity of 52,000 tons of refined sugar. Present Ethiopian consumption is somewhat less than half this figure. Eventually, when domestic sugar production has been further expanded, all domestic requirements can be met without the need for imports, with perhaps even a moderate exportable surplus.

Most of the industrial establishments in the Empire are concentrated in and around Addis Ababa and Asmara. A few are at Dire Dawa, a few others at Massawa and elsewhere in Eritrea; a number of coffee-hulling and-cleaning establishments are found in the interior.

No reliable figures are available on the nationality of the capital invested in Ethiopian industry. In Eritrea it may be assumed from the names of the entrepreneurs that over 90 per cent of the capital invested is Italian. In Addis Ababa most of it is Armenian and Greek. The investment of A. Besse and Company, the country's largest exporter and importer, as well as its largest coffee and grain processer, is French. There is also some small-scale Italian enterprise, notably one tomato-canning establishment at Shashamana, and mechanical work and repair shops. American capital has made many inquiries but has yet to make its appearance in a productive capacity. The only significant American investment to date is that of Sinclair Oil, which for ten years or so was engaged in exploratory oil drilling operations— without success—in the Ogaden. A Swiss-Israeli firm operates meat-packing, canning, and freezing facilities at Asmara, and has sought permission to set up similar facilities at Dire Dawa, on the railway to Djibouti. Yugoslav capital has been invested in a sawmill and lumbering concession in Jimma province, in retail distribution facilities at Addis Ababa, and most recently, on a very large scale, in a harbor improvement project at Assab.

Little Ethiopian capital is invested in industry, partly because there is not much to invest, but also because of the traditional Ethiopian distrust of business and commerce. Leaving aside for the moment the investment in public utilities, transportation, and communications, Ethiopian capital (largely government capital) has gone primarily into cigarette manufacture, slaughtering, baking, cement manufacture, and cotton textile production. There is also a government munitions factory. The cement factory and the cotton factory, both at Dire Dawa,[1] were originally Italian enterprises; they were expropriated by the Ethiopian government at the end of the war. The Tobacco Monopoly is likewise a government venture. Private Ethiopian capital participation in industry is probably not in excess of a few million Ethiopian dollars.

[1] A second, smaller, cotton factory was erected at Addis Ababa in 1954 and during 1956 a third was reported to be under construction in Eritrea. As mentioned earlier, an Indian firm expects to erect another.

The output of industry in Ethiopia is another matter on which accurate information is very difficult to obtain. The Ministry of Commerce and Industry has made several praiseworthy attempts to gather such information, but its figures are incomplete and many of them are only estimates. Furthermore, the published results of such preliminary inquiries as have been made exclude Eritrean data. Regular reporting of industrial production, of employment, of wages and salaries, of hours worked, and so on, is far from the habit in Ethiopia as yet, and the limited staff and funds available for this important task make it difficult, at present, to do much more.[2]

The results of the Ministry's preliminary survey of industry, published in March 1956, are summarized briefly in what follows.

It appears that in Ethiopia proper the number of industrial establishments of all kinds increased from approximately 107 in 1951 to 172 in 1954, the latest year of the census. (The latter figure, it will be noted, is considerably larger than the total of 136 industrial establishments listed for Ethiopia in the same ministry's 1955 publication, *Economic Progress of Ethiopia*.) The increase was due mainly to a rise in the number of coffee-and grain-cleaning establishments in operation during these years. But the ministry immediately qualifies the printed results with the statement that the figures should not be held to be exact.

The numbers employed in Ethiopian industry (including electric light and power but not mining and construction) increased from approximately 7,000 in 1951 to over 12,000 in 1954, according to the same survey. The 1954 figure includes 500-odd foreigners, nearly all of them in key positions. The increases were mainly in coffee and grain-cleaning establishments (few of which existed in the earlier year), and in sugar, textile, and vegetable oil factories.

Total sales of Ethiopian industry (excluding mining and construction) were approximately Eth.$44.6 million in 1954, compared with Eth.$28.1 million in 1951. About 82 per cent of the 1954 total were sales of manufacturing industry, the rest of coffee- and grain-cleaning

[2] Other statistical ventures should unquestionably be given higher priority—e.g., the initiation of some form of farm crop reporting.

establishments and of light and power. In manufacturing, the largest contributor to the total product is the food-processing industry (vegetable oil and soap, flour, sugar, and tomato canning), which accounted for approximately 37 per cent of the total in 1954. Next largest is the textile industry, with a little less than a third of the total. The rest is largely accounted for by sawmills, leather and shoe factories, cement and brick manufacture, tobacco production, and distilling.

Annual capital expenditure of industry in Ethiopia is very low, being limited almost wholly to replacement needs. With the important exception of the large new investment in sugar, such investment has been limited to between two and three million Ethiopian dollars per annum in recent years. These figures, again, exclude Eritrea, for which data are even less accessible than for Ethiopia, but in any case the combined total is probably not in excess of Eth.$8 million.

Wages paid by manufacturing industry in Ethiopia are very low by Western standards, but about double the average per capita income for the country as a whole. The latter has been estimated at between Eth.$150 and Eth.$200 per annum (U.S.$60 to U.S.$80). Such statistics as there are on this subject, again from the Ministry of Commerce, indicate an upward trend in manufacturing wages during recent years. Administrative and technical staff, mostly non-Ethiopian, receive salaries ten and fifteen times as high as ordinary workers, with a few top officials earning much more. As already indicated, such staff number less than 5 per cent of all industrial employees.

Trade unionism is in its most elementary stages in Ethiopia. Social and political awareness is still very rudimentary, where it exists at all. However, there have been some instances of strikes, notably of dock workers in Eritrea. Employees of the Franco-Ethiopian Railroad (which has had a trade union since 1947) have struck twice, ostensibly for higher wages. In October 1957 a strike of Eritrean workers was threatened—and averted only by warnings of police action—to force promulgation of a labor code that had been passed by the Eritrean legislative assembly but blocked by the Emperor's Representative in Eritrea, who may have feared that such a law in Eritrea would lead to agitation for a similar law in Ethiopia proper. Generally, however, strikes have been ineffective and rare.

Factory conditions are very crude and simple, with some notable exceptions, as in the new tobacco factory at Addis Ababa, where modern equipment, good organization, and cleanliness prevail. Even the crudest factory conditions, however, are generally superior to the conditions of the average worker's home, and hence do not occasion any grievance.

There are few data on the number of hours worked in industry. The eight-hour day and the six-day week, however, are general, and may be taken as standard. Industrial productivity, or output per man-hour, is very low, thanks largely to outmoded equipment, inefficient management, and unskilled, apathetic workers. Absenteeism is high, and disciplinary action is useless because the condition is so general.[3] The problem of migratory labor, so important in some other parts of Africa, scarcely affects Ethiopian industry. Workers are usually permanently settled near where they work.

Ethiopian workers are in general easy to teach, but slow to comprehend. They usually think they have mastered the job after they have become accustomed to the routine and gathered a smattering of technical knowledge. Most of them have a poorly developed sense of responsibility by Western standards, and consequently tend to be deplorably careless with tools and machinery. In jobs entailing responsibility for life and limb, such as aircraft repair, it has been repeatedly confirmed that Ethiopians cannot be entrusted with final responsibility for safety. The excellent record of Ethiopian Airlines is an impressive one, but the credit belongs to the American and other foreign maintenance staff, not to the Ethiopian mechanics-in-training. The fact is that, after twelve full years of training and preparation, the government itself does not yet feel that full and complete responsibility for airline operation and maintenance can be entrusted to its own people.

In the public utility and communications field most of the groundwork was laid during the Italian occupation.[4] Very few roads, tele-

---

[3] It must be remembered also that the Ethiopian worker, being able to fall back on numerous outside means of support, may not be as dependent on his job as workers in Western countries.

[4] With the notable exception of the railroad from Djibouti to Addis Ababa, which was completed in 1917.

phones, or electric power stations existed in Ethiopia before 1935. Italy's investment in roadbuilding alone is stated to have been between £80 million and £100 million,[5] and as much or more may have been spent on developing the telegraph and telephone system, on hydroelectric facilities, and on other public construction.

Ethiopia's postwar prosperity and economic expansion permitted the government to build on this broad base of initial investment and to extend it considerably. No figures are available on the production of electricity during the Italian occupation, but from 1948 to 1955 electric light and power output in Ethiopia proper more than doubled, from 13.4 million kilowatt hours to 27.8 million.[6] In addition, an estimated 10 million KWH were self-produced by industry in 1955 because of the inability of the Ethiopian Electric Light and Power Company to comply with the total demand. Some two dozen communities within the empire are now served by electric power, and consumption continues to grow.

The aggregate rated capacity of public power facilities in Ethiopia at the beginning of 1956 was 14,292 kilovolt amperes, 58 per cent of which was hydroelectric and the rest thermal. To alleviate the perennial power shortage in the Addis Ababa area, four 250-k.v.a. diesel units were installed during 1955, and by the middle of 1957 a further 5,000 k.v.a. were in operation. Italian war reparations will pay for the enlarging of a small dam at Koka, on the Awash River, about eighty kilometers southeast of Addis Ababa, which is expected to furnished an additional 10,000 k.v.a. by 1961.

Eritrea has its own installations, estimated to have produced 22.5 million KWH in 1950, 90 per cent of which was thermal.[7] Current output is reportedly somewhat less than this, owing to the departure of additional numbers of Italians since federation and the decline in economic activity.

The policy of the Ethiopian government toward private capital investment has been made somewhat more inviting in recent years,

[5] Perham, *The Government of Ethiopia*, p. 182.
[6] Almost 90 per cent of this consumption is in Addis Ababa.
[7] Report of the United Nations Commission for Eritrea (New York, 1950), p. 14.

but has succeeded in attracting little actual capital. There has been a good deal of preliminary interest on the part of potential investors, but for one reason or another—prejudice against business, suspicion of foreigners, fear of exploitation—their proposals have nearly all come to naught. To judge from the accounts of several disgruntled would-be investors, the government's approach to their proposals has been disorganized and immature; applications have been treated not so much on their merits as on such intangible factors as the applicant's personality; other applications have been altogether ignored; still others have given rise to endless delay and bickering. All this has understandably exhausted the patience of numerous investors, who have subsequently withdrawn their proposals. One suspects that the loser, in all cases or nearly all, has been Ethiopia.

The basic document on which Ethiopia's investment policy nominally rests is Legal Notice No. 10 of 1950, entitled Statement of Policy for the Encouragement of Foreign Capital Investment in Ethiopia. The points of this statement may be summarized briefly: (1) new enterprises to be free from the payment of profit tax for five years from the date production begins; (2) the importation of machinery for factory installation in such enterprises to be free from the payment of customs duties; (3) Ethiopian capital participation, in general, not to be imposed on new enterprises; (4) dividend and interest payments abroad to be permitted within limits; (5) the complete withdrawal of invested capital to be permitted only gradually.

The first two points of this statement are seemingly unequivocal. The last three are hedged about, in the actual statement, with qualifications that leave investors uncertain about what specific benefits they may expect under these provisions. Regardless of this declaration of policy, the actual terms of the foreign investment will depend exclusively on the contract the investor concludes with the Ethiopian government.[8] The policy of the government does not permit the

---

[8] As a practical matter, investors should be wary of concluding contracts exclusively with private sources in Ethiopia, i.e., without the knowledge and approval of the government, not because of possible default on the part of private sources but because the investor's definition of his rights under such a contract may not square with the government's.

ownership of real property by foreigners; however, long-term leases are possible. There are no stated restrictions on the proportion of foreign capital participation in an enterprise, or on the control of management. There are likewise no explicit restrictions on the employment of foreign technicians and workers. There are no special taxes levied on foreign investments exclusively.

Arbitrary legal action by the government, as in the 1955 cases of ex post facto taxation of numerous small businesses and private individuals in Addis Ababa, can probably be discounted by the foreign investor with a firm contract, rigorously defined, and substantial invested capital. Foreign investors need also have no great concern over the stability of the government as long as the present Emperor is on the throne. The country's ample foreign exchange reserves make it likely that no barriers will be erected to the transfer of interest, dividends, or capital abroad within the limits of the official agreement, at least in the near future.

One major investment project in the transportation field is of French, not Italian origin. This is the Chemin de Fer Franco-Ethiopien de Djibouti à Addis Abeba, more popularly known as the C.F.E. or the Franco-Ethiopian Railroad, begun in 1897 under the reign of Menelik and completed in 1917. It is the only railway in Ethiopia proper. Its total distance is 486 miles and it is of meter gauge, in contrast to Eritrea's Italian-built railway (from Massawa to Asmara and beyond to Bisha, 224 miles in all), which is of 95-centimeter gauge. The original investment by the French was 17.3 million gold francs, equivalent at today's depreciated rates to about U.S.$50,000.[9] The same railroad could probably not be built today for less than a quarter of a billion dollars. Depreciation in the line and its rolling stock has, of course, been substantial, and its equipment is in many cases obsolete. Still, next to the road system it represents today the most important foreign investment in Ethiopia, and it is one of the country's chief economic assets. It carries annually some 40 to 50 per cent of the country's freight, amounting in 1955 to 255,000 tons, compared

[9] Even this is excessive if the August, 1957, de facto devaluation of the franc is taken into account.

to an average of well under 100,000 tons in the decade preceding the liberation of 1941.

The Ethiopian government benefits from the operations of the railway to the extent of a quarter interest in the original investment, plus an annual return of 20 per cent of the net profit after deduction of interest and replacement charges. (The 20 per cent is calculated only on net earnings over the section of the line that runs through Ethiopian territory, which is some seven-eighths of the total length.) The postwar profits of the railway company, computed in depreciated francs on the original investment, have been meager indeed, and in 1950, 1954, and 1955 the company reported a substantial loss, despite the fact that its rates are reputed to be the highest in the world. Competition from road transportation has been increasing since the highway renovation program began in early 1951, and the railway has been forced to make successive reductions in its rates to keep them competitive with road haulage. The future of the railroad is not promising, as roads and highways become further developed and extended. Ethiopia seems to have bypassed the railroad age in its development, and the excessive cost of constructing new and additional rail lines today, compared with the cost of highway construction, makes the C.F.E.'s resurgence most unlikely.

The U.S.$24 million Eximbank loan referred to earlier[10] seems disproportionate to Ethiopia's present investment in aviation property and equipment, which is less than 15 per cent of the principal involved, as well as to the needs of aviation development itself. In partial support of this statement, it appears that very little of the credit has been drawn upon up to the present time. It is true that air transportation has played an increasingly important part in the economic life of the country and that present facilities are strained, but a much smaller loan would probably have been entirely adequate to relieve the situation.

In any case, air transportation in Ethiopia has assumed its present importance only because there are no roads, relatively speaking. This form of transportation can never hope to replace, or even to compete

[10] See Chapter V, p. 67.

seriously with, surface transportation on a long-term basis.[11] The 1951 IBRD loan of U.S.$5 million for highway rehabilitation and maintenance (and even the latest of $15 million) seems puny alongside the aviation loan—especially when we recall that the total investment in Ethiopian roads is some Eth.$1½ billion, at present replacement cost.

Under the terms of the highway loan agreement entered into between Ethiopia and the IBRD in September 1950,[12] an autonomous Imperial Highway Authority was set up in Addis Ababa to supervise the rehabilitation and maintenance of the country's 4,100 kilometers of primary roads (excluding Eritrea). The foreign exchange proceeds of the loan have been used to help finance services and to purchase equipment and imported materials for the program. Local currency costs have been met by the Ethiopian government.

When the Highway Authority began operations in the spring of 1951, it was found that the condition of the roads was generally much worse than had been anticipated when the loan was granted. Very little maintenance work had been performed for a number of years prior to 1951, and as a result side drainage ditches and culvert inlets and outlets had become filled and vegetation had grown over them to such an extent that they had almost completely ceased to function. Surface water was seriously eroding the roadway. There were innumerable cases of base and subgrade failures. Bituminous paving was generally in poor condition. Many retaining walls, bridges, and other structures had failed, or were on the verge of failing. Roads were in many places deeply rutted, sometimes so badly as to make them impassable. The Highway Authority's annual report for 1953 states bluntly: "During the early days of the IHA the term maintenance was a misnomer, as there was but little to maintain." For some time the Highway Authority undertook only essential work of an emergency nature and actual reconstruction work.

With the small amount of capital at its disposal, the Highway Authority has done a commendable job. Judging from the statistics

---

[11] On a volume basis less than 2 per cent of the country's freight is carried by air.

[12] See Chapter V, pp. 66–67.

it cites in its fourth annual report, dated February 28, 1955, it accomplished in its first three years the limited objectives it had set for that period. These were to reconstruct three main roads (Addis Ababa to Assab, Addis Ababa to Jimma, and Addis Ababa to Lekempti), covering 1,469 kilometers of the 4,100-kilometer primary system, and to maintain the balance of the system "to permit travel . . . and to prevent further deterioration." Much of the credit must go to the efficient American administration and the autonomous nature of the Authority. Nevertheless, some of the main roads even today are far from first-class, and trucks still bog down in the mud in many places during the rainy season.

There are other problems besides the weather. For example, despite the Highway Authority's repeated urging on the basis of traffic counts and load studies it has made, the Ethiopian government has still not enacted any legislation to limit the weights of vehicles. Sample weighing operations indicate that a large number of trucks now on the road exceed the recommended axle load limit of eight metric tons. Many of them, including fuel tankers on which it is difficult to reduce total loads, carry axle loads in excess of ten metric tons.

The road program carried out to date, though in general satisfactory from the standpoint of the funds originally made available by the IBRD, is far too small in relation to the needs of the country, estimated by the director of the IHA in October 1955 at some 16,000 kilometers of first-class roads, about four times the present total. The 1957 IBRD loan will help toward this goal.

After the foreign exchange proceeds of the first loan were entirely disbursed (end of May, 1954), the Ethiopian government bore the entire cost of the road program under an agreement with the United States Bureau of Public Roads to supply management personnel. Up to the end of February, 1955, that is, during the initial four years of the first road program, the IHA's total outlays amounted to some Eth. $42 million, of which some 55 per cent was in foreign exchange. The IBRD loan of the equivalent of Eth.$12.5 million represented about 30 per cent of this total. The Ethiopian government agreed to provide an additional Eth.$20 million for the two years from March 1, 1955, to February 28, 1957, for maintenance of the entire network, now including approximately 900 kilometers in Eritrea, and for further improvement of some of the roads. The maintenance funds were reported to be barely adequate to meet minimum requirements.

The IHA has had certain difficulties in carrying out its operations in the interior, among them labor problems, armed attacks, and opposition from some provincial governors, who would like the roads to pass near their own property. The Gallas around Lekempti, on the Assab road, and near Shashamana refuse to accept employment on the roads; money means nothing to them ("Their wives support them," remarked the director, "while the little kids tend the herds"). Somalis are employed as truck drivers "because they don't drink." There were *shifta* (armed bandits) causing trouble in Eritrea early in 1955. Other armed attacks have taken place at IHA camps, along the Assab road (where sixteen policemen had to be employed for protection after one murderous attack), in the Takazze area in Begemder province, and elsewhere. There has also been difficulty in getting the Ethiopian government to realize that when a road has been built the work is not over—that maintenance is just as important.

The effects of the highway improvement program show up in the steady growth of road traffic, in the substantial reduction of both truck and rail transportation rates, and in a large increase in imports of motor vehicles and fuel. The value of imports handled at the port of Assab, which is served only by highway, more than doubled between 1953 and 1955, compared with a much smaller increase in imports as a whole. Despite its wholly inadequate facilities (which are now being expanded), this port is now handling, in volume, about 80 per cent as much traffic as Djibouti, a far superior port in French Somaliland connected by rail with the Ethiopian hinterland. Nevertheless, at present traffic on almost all rural roads is below 100 vehicles a day, in both directions, and on most of them it is far below this. For all its improvements and promise, Ethiopia is a land in which roads of any sort are still a relative novelty, and well over three-fourths of the produce of the country is still carried to market over rough trails by packhorse, mule, and donkey.

Air transportation, as we have seen, has nowhere near the importance, economically speaking, of surface transport. Ethiopian Airlines, Inc., the national airline founded in 1945, has a monopoly of the domestic routes but carries less than 2 per cent of the country's export and import tonnage. In 1955 EAL's freight tonnage flown was less than 5,000 tons out of a total estimated rail, truck, and air tonnage of some 335,000 tons. The total investment in air transportation facilities in Ethiopia was Eth.$7.8 million at the end of 1955. This figure represents the assets of Ethiopian Airlines, including the company's twelve aircraft, nine DC-3s, and three Convair 240s. Routes flown include about two dozen Ethiopian centers and some half dozen foreign cities, from Nairobi in the south to Athens in the north. In early 1956 Ethiopian Airlines was flying to Athens six times a week. The line operates under an agreement with TWA (Trans-World Airlines), which for a fee of U.S.$25,000 a year furnishes management and technical personnel. The arrangement was made in 1945 and has twice been renewed, in 1953 and again in 1956. Pilots are American, but Ethiopians have been trained as radio operators and copilots and have in recent years been introduced on international as well as on national routes. The government expects that Ethiopian pilots will someday completely replace foreign pilots on the airline. Ethiopian Airlines has had a good safety record since the start of its operations in early 1946: not a single fatality in the approximately 140 million passenger miles flown in its first decade. Air transportation has brought Ethiopia into the twentieth century as has no other medium, all but eliminating her isolation from neighboring states and the world. Yet it cannot be more than an interim solution for real development, which must lie in the direction of surface transportation, and particularly in roads.

As we have seen, the IBRD granted two other development loans to Ethiopia in 1950–51, one of them for the expansion of telecommunications facilities. Under it an Imperial Board of Telecommunications was set up to operate Ethiopia's telecommunications services and carry out a program for their expansion and improvement. Its members, like those of the Imperial Highway Authority, were selected by the Ethiopian government in cooperation with the IBRD. The board was slow in getting started; no withdrawals were made under the loan until more than three years after the signing of the loan agreement, and less than two-thirds of the principal amount granted under the loan (U.S.$1½ million) had been expended up to the closing date—several times extended—of December 31, 1955. Like the highway loan, the telecommunications loan was used to finance the purchase of equipment, services, and supplies from overseas. The Telecommunications Board would, in the opinion of the International Bank, function more efficiently if its Ethiopian board of directors gave more active support to the management and took a more active interest in the formulation of policy.

According to the latest estimates, the total cost of the IBTE's investment program up to the closing date of the loan amounted to about Eth.$7.5 million, of which about Eth.$5.0 million was in foreign exchange. Three-fourths of the foreign exchange cost was to have been met by the International Bank loan and the rest by the conversion of local currency. The investment program does not include rehabilitation and maintenance, which are classed as operating expenditure, nor does it cover Eritrea, for which investment expenditures have been included in IBTE's new three-year program, which began in 1956.

Progress made thus far under the telecommunications loan covers four main fields: (1) Addis Ababa telephone exchanges and network; (2) provincial telephone services; (3) domestic telegraph system; and (4) international telecommunications services. Before the reconstruction work started early in 1953, Addis Ababa was served by an old automatic exchange with a capacity of 1,500 lines. Owing to lack of maintenance, however, about 35 per cent of the calls went wrong within the exchange and there were some two hundred complaints daily about other matters. The provincial network (excluding Eritrea) had only three towns equipped with telephone exchanges, all of obsolete type and badly in need of repair. In addition, some fifty towns had telephone connections, but they were out of service most of the time. Only fifteen towns had direct telegraph service, with messages transmitted at hand speed and frequently garbled. The equipment was largely obsolete.

IBTE's accomplishments to date include the installation of two new automatic exchanges for Addis Ababa, with a capacity of 4,300 lines, the overhauling of the subsurface and wire network, the expansion and overhauling of interurban exchanges and networks and the introduction in several towns of new or overhauled manual exchanges, the installation of radio-telephone links between major centers as a reserve in the event of line failure, the overhauling of the Addis Ababa radio station, and the opening of direct telegraph and telephone service to Europe.

The third IBRD loan was for the establishment of an Ethiopian Development Bank. This institution was set up in March 1951 as an instrumentality of the Ethiopian government, in order to assist in the development of agricultural and industrial production and to stimulate the use of private capital for productive purposes. The bank was established ostensibly because of the lack of adequate financial institutions for the making of reasonable loans for development. The management is European but the board, again, is Ethiopian.

The capital stock of the Development Bank was authorized at Eth.$13 million. Of this, $11 million represented the ordinary capital stock, to be subscribed by the Ethiopian government; the remaining $2 million was to be offered for sale either for public or private subscription when authorized by the board (up to the end of 1957 no such authorization had been given). Of the $11 million subscribed by the government, $2 million was paid in immediately in cash; $3 million was to be payable on call of the board; $1 million was paid in the form of capital assets of the previously existing Agricultural and Commercial Bank of Ethiopia on its merger with the Development Bank; and the remaining $5 million was to be treated as a counterpart of the U.S.$2 million loan from the IBRD. The Ethiopian government was to receive shares of stock in fulfillment of its subscription equivalent to the amounts withdrawn from the IBRD loan account. As of December 31, 1957, the paid-in capital of the Development Bank amounted to Eth.$10.0 million, of which Eth.$6.0 million had been paid in by the Ethiopian government and the rest by the IBRD. Under the loan agreement the U.S.$2 million was provided to finance the foreign exchange costs of projects supported by the IBRD. This loan, like the others by the International Bank, carries an interest rate of 4 per cent (including commission) and is repayable within twenty years, with payments beginning in 1956.

Up to the end of 1955 a little less than two-thirds of the loan funds had been expended. Outstanding on the books of the Development Bank at that time were some Eth.$7.5 million of agricultural and industrial loans, of which total industrial loans comprised about 62 per cent. The Development Bank, like the Telecommunications Board, was slow in getting started and operated at a loss for the first two years. In order to equip itself with some earning assets, the demand for loans being very low, the bank was obliged to create an operating subsidiary, the Ceres Company, which handles a commission and financing business in cereals, oilseeds, and pulses. Starting in 1953, however, the bank began earning a profit on its loan operations, owing in part to an increase in loan activity and in part to economies in personnel expenditure.

Since 1952 investments in agricultural loans have risen more rapidly than in industrial loans, although the latter are still in a majority. Individual industrial loans have been much bigger than agricultural loans, averaging a little less than Eth.$80,000 up to the end of 1955, compared with about Eth.$2,600 for agricultural loans. Up to the end of 1955 about eighty-five industrial development loans had been extended by the bank in such diverse fields as cotton textile production, food processing (macaroni, oils, and meat), plant fiber extraction, and shoe and leather manufacture; 724 loans of much smaller average size had been made to agriculture, including 133 for coffee development. A smaller number of others, averaging some Eth. $8,000 each, had been granted against personal or title deed guarantee.

In agriculture the low level of education among applicants, the lack of research, and the nonexistence of extension services have been limitations on the planning of any satisfactory development projects for financing. Legal difficulties, especially the difficulty of establishing clear identification of ownership to real property, have also proved severe handicaps to the bank's operations in this field. There are many areas of the country where no individual property, in the Western sense, exists. In rural districts in the north the family or clan is the property-owning entity, and in the south grants of a feudal character still exist. Title deeds are rare. Under these conditions it is difficult to establish firmly the debtor's legal obligation under a credit by the bank. Small agricultural loans are, in fact, granted only in Shoa province, where the law of land ownership makes possible a satisfactory guarantee. Agricultural loans are most often used by the borrowers for the purchase of livestock, and sometimes for simple equipment.

Loans to both industry and agriculture have suffered from the shortage of profitable and clearly defined investment opportunities. Loans have been fairly few and relatively small, contradicting the old wheeze that all countries at Ethiopia's stage of development have vast opportunities for investment but lack the necessary capital. The lack of profitable opportunities is, in turn, a reflection on the nature of Ethiopian society, the low level of Ethiopian education, transportation, and communication, and the character of the people.

One problem has been the business attitudes of Ethiopian entrepreneurs. With few exceptions, businessmen in Ethiopia in 1951 were not acquainted with the technique of business term loans. They were used to short-term loans with fixed maturity, subject to extension, overdraft credit, and credit against notes and documents. Through the Development Bank the principle is being slowly established that loans may be linked to special projects and funds disbursed only for agreed expenditure. It has been difficult to overcome the reluctance of businessmen to divulge accurate accounting information; what they supply along these lines is frequently primitive, when they supply anything at all. Businessmen have been wont to consider any progress reports, inventory checks, or computation of depreciation allowances as unnecessary nuisances. These attitudes have considerably hampered the functioning of the Development Bank.

Because the Development Bank, according to its terms of reference, has to be self-supporting, it has had to reject many applications which were inadequately formulated, and others because the applicant's credit reputation was unfavorable, his project unworkable, or his true financial position doubtful. The volume of applications rejected on these and related grounds has been large enough to raise the question of to what extent the Development Bank should assist the applicant in preparing a sound application. Even where an applicant comes in with an unrealistic proposition, the bank might conceivably divert his attention to more fruitful fields, especially if he has managerial talent and some resources of his own. The Development Bank has been reluctant, however, to take such initiative where its own staff would have to take any large responsibility for working up plans, partly because its staff is limited but also because it believes that a development credit institution would be unwise to make the kind of advance commitment which the assigning of its own staff might imply. Although this is sound policy, it raises a serious problem in a country where the small entrepreneurs are relatively inexperienced and have great difficulty in securing access to technical advice.

Perhaps the most imaginative and farthest-reaching of the post-war development projects in Ethiopia has been the Point Four program, operating under the United States International Cooperation Administration. Point Four aid to foreign countries has as its main purpose the economic and social betterment of underdeveloped areas, which it attempts to achieve through technical advice and active assistance in cooperative projects with the governments of such countries. However, the program is not entirely altruistic. The reward to the giver, the United States, is calculated in terms of political good will and improved trade prospects.

The Point Four program in Ethiopia began in May 1952, and now embraces projects in the fields of agriculture, water resources, education (including general, technical, science, agricultural, handicraft, and vocational), public health and sanitation, commerce and industry, and public administration. The United States furnishes the specialists and the Ethiopian government the other personnel, the land, the buildings, and other contributions for the various projects. In most projects operating costs are shared equally through the medium of special "joint funds."

The main feature of the Point Four program is training. The idea is to develop a native corps of trained technical and administrative personnel capable of assuming, eventually, full responsibility for the operation and management of development projects. In addition to on-the-job training, the program attempts to achieve this long-term objective by helping to expand and improve the country's existing institutions which can provide such training. If facilities for training are not available within the country, promising young native personnel may be sent abroad for study.

The many activities that have been undertaken by the Point Four program in Ethiopia are too numerous and varied to permit of detailed description here. Its personnel have helped set up several agricultural technical schools including the one at Jimma, an agricultural improvement center, an agricultural machinery pool, plant protection and pest control, cooperative coffee development, and animal disease control. They have conducted a water resources survey (notably in the Lake Tana–Blue Nile region) and a well-drilling program. They have set up a cooperative education program, designed to assist the government in developing a modern educational program and school system adapted to the needs of the country. They have established a "public health college" and training center, a nurse and midwife training school, a nurse education program, and health and advisory services. They carried out a water and sewage survey. They set up a commerce and industry development service (discontinued in 1956), providing technological information and advice to businessmen and prospective investors. They reorganized the Addis Ababa handicraft school and set up provincial handicraft centers. They carried out studies to improve the organization and quality of government administrative processes and services.

Up to the end of 1956 the United States had spent approximately $11.5 million in its combined Point Four operations in Ethiopia and Eritrea. At that time a renewal and extension of the program was announced.[18] Modest though its activities are in relation to the potential needs of the country, the Point Four program is undoubtedly contributing to Ethiopian development in the most helpful manner. It is bringing a breath of fresh air and American business efficiency to the country. It is attacking the problem of raising the standard of living of a primitive people in the way best calculated to produce last-

[18] Some 130 American technicians were engaged in these operations in 1958, chiefly in the fields of agriculture, education, and public health.

ing results, i.e. by education and training, not by massive capital investments. The Point Four program in Ethiopia has also produced some good will for America among Ethiopians. On the negative side, it must be said that Point Four personnel have complained of the slowness and inefficiency of certain Ethiopian authorities, and of the positive obstructionism of a few who have a vested interest in the status quo.

Although Ethiopia has more than a dozen rivers, none is navigable except the Baro in the west, and then only a short distance inland to Gambeila for several months of the year at the height of the rains. In a country where the lack of good roads and the mountainous terrain make communication difficult, the absence of navigable streams places an added handicap on transportation. Many of the rivers, moreover, are short and precipitous, and some of them are dry for the greater part of the year. They have thus played almost no part in the country's economic development to date, except to a limited degree for irrigation and for the production of hydroelectric power.

During their occupation of Ethiopia the Italians carried out extensive water resources surveys, but their records have been lost, and Point Four, which is now engaged in this field, has had to start from scratch in measuring river water flow and ground water supplies. A small dam at Koka, on the Awash River, started but never completed by the Italians, is now scheduled for completion and enlargement by the Ethiopian government, with the help of Italian reparations and Point Four technical advice. Next to nothing is known about any of the other rivers.[14] Even at Koka, lack of sufficient data on water flow has held up progress. When it is known how many cubic meters of water are available at any point on a river at different seasons, it becomes possible, in conjunction with known requirements for different crops, to plan an irrigation program. Otherwise too much water may be taken out of the river. An absolute prerequisite for large-scale irrigation and hydroelectric development schemes is a long-range water resources survey program, which must be con-

[14] Considerable water flow and other hydrological data are available on the Blue Nile, in which the British have long been interested.

tinually maintained. Aside from some local irrigation that is practiced wherever water can be diverted into fields without much difficulty, not even a start has been made in this direction. Lake Tana in the north could become the source of a vast hydroelectric and irrigation development, but nothing except vague talk has been heard about this project of projects for over fifty years.[15]

In regard to mineral wealth, no definite estimate of Ethiopia's resources has ever been made and there has been practically no attempt to exploit the known deposits. Gold is found in the Sidamo, Wollega, and Gojjam provinces, and platinum in Wollega. Lignite is also found in Wollega, in the Nejjo district, in parts of Shoa, and in the Lake Tana area. There are said to be nonferrous metals in various parts of the country, but so far none are mined. There are also said to be traces of copper, tin, lead, tungsten, cobalt, and molybdenum. The Chercher mountains, west of Harar, are believed to hold deposits of copper and lead. Mica exists near Nejjo in Wollega. Graphite of good quality has been discovered near Harar. Salt is being mined in the Danakil desert, and other salt deposits have been reported near Mega on the Kenya border.

At present gold, salt, and a little platinum are the only minerals being worked in Ethiopia and Eritrea. Adola, in the south of Ethiopia, is the only gold field (apart from a few scattered mines in Eritrea) now being worked on a production basis, and this largely with convict labor. Some U.S.$300,000 was spent on mining machinery for the Adola operation, in an effort to double the output obtainable by traditional hand digging methods, but obstructionism in high places, lack of spare parts for the machinery at Adola, and dissent among the foreign staff assigned to the operation have combined to bring the whole plan to nought. There was no evidence, five years after the installation of modern equipment and the "mechanization" of the operation, that gold production in Ethiopia was any greater

---

[15] In 1957 it was announced that yet another survey of the Blue Nile, which originates in Lake Tana and flows into the Nile proper, was to be undertaken, by means of aerial photography. This joint U.S.-Ethiopian project was to be conducted under the auspices of Point Four, the U.S. Bureau of Reclamation, and the U.S. Coast and Geodetic Survey.

than it had ever been. In the period 1945–50 this was about 50,000 crude troy ounces per year. If anything, it appears that production has fallen to half or less than half of its former level, judging by the records on gold entering the Ethiopian Treasury. Certainly there were no gold exports from Ethiopia in 1953–55, whereas in the period 1945–50 such exports averaged more than 60 per cent of total production. An Imperial Ethiopian Mining Board, set up in 1953 ostensibly to promote the exploration of the country's mineral wealth and to develop mining operations, collapsed less than two years later. In 1955 an American firm was granted a large mining concession and exclusive prospecting rights in certain parts of the country (oil excepted).

The Sinclair Oil Company of America sank almost U.S.$10 million into oil exploration in southeastern Ethiopia before pulling up stakes. The company had a fifty-year concession agreement with the Ethiopian government and exclusive rights to operations in any part of the country, Eritrea apparently excepted. Despite intensive operations over a ten-year period, during which some seventeen wells were drilled, including two over 10,000 feet deep, no oil was found, although one well showed some traces of hydrocarbons. The discovery of oil in Ethiopia would have brought a great many changes, not all of them, perhaps, for the better.

X

Eritrea

The territory of Eritrea, bounded on the south by Ethiopia, on the west by the Sudan, and on the north and east by the Red Sea, was integrated into the Empire of Ethiopia under a unique federal arrangement by United Nations action on September 15, 1952. Prior to that date it had been administered for eleven years by Great Britain, after the collapse of the Italian East African Empire in 1941, and for half a century before that by Italy. Ethiopia's claim to it, and the basis on which it was eventually restored to its southern neighbor, rested partly on historical, geographical, political, and ethnic grounds. The story is long and obscure; Ethiopia's claims were perhaps never as strong as official propaganda made them out to be. For several thousand years Ethiopia had exercised a shadowy suzerainty over parts of the territory to which Italy gave the name of Eritrea in 1890, but for long periods of time Ethiopian control was at most nominal. Italy's encroachments in this area in the nineteenth century were at the expense not of Ethiopia, but of Egypt, which had previously wrested control from Turkey.

Eritrea, under Italian rule, developed economically and politically much more rapidly than Ethiopia, and it today occupies a special place in the political structure of the Ethiopian Empire quite different from that of any province. Technically, it constitutes an "autonomous unit federated with Ethiopia under the sovereignty of the Ethiopian Crown."[1]

[1] Federal Act between Ethiopia and Eritrea, para. 1.

Unlike other parts of the Empire, it possesses "legislative, executive and judicial powers in the field of domestic affairs."[2] There is a popularly elected Eritrean Assembly, which reflects in its composition the religious and political sentiments of the territory, and which chooses its own Chief Executive. The jurisdiction of the Federal government (the Ethiopian government) extends only to defense, foreign affairs, currency and finance, foreign and interstate commerce, and external and internal communications, including ports. The Federal government has the power to maintain the integrity of the federation and to impose uniform taxes to meet the expenses of federal functions and services. The jurisdiction of the Eritrean government is, in theory, analogous to that of the American states, being one of residual powers, except that the United States federal government is a distinct entity separate from and superior to the governments of any of the constituent parts. The Eritrean government's jurisdiction extends to all matters not expressly vested in the Federal government by the act of federation (known as the Federal Act), including the power to maintain the internal police, to levy taxes to meet domestic expenses, and to adopt its own budget.

The same Federal Act states that Ethiopia and Eritrea shall constitute a single customs area; that a single nationality shall prevail throughout the federation; that Eritrean citizens shall participate in the executive and judicial branches, and shall be represented in the legislative branch of the Federal government "in accordance with law and in the proportion that the population of Eritrea bears to the population of the Federation";[3] that an Imperial Federal Council, composed of equal numbers of Ethiopians and Eritreans, shall meet at least once a year to "advise" upon the common affairs of the federation; and that the Federal government, as well as the Eritrean government, shall ensure to residents in Eritrea without distinction of nationality, race, sex, language, or religion the enjoyment of certain fundamental human rights and liberties.

Eritrea has its own constitution, a remarkably democratic document when contrasted with that of Ethiopia. The latter is a strange

[2] *Ibid.*, para. 2.
[3] *Ibid.*, para. 5. Neither population is accurately known.

composite of monarchical tradition and western parliamentary concepts, drawn up chiefly by an American adviser to the Emperor. The former, on the other hand, is entirely devoid of political anachronisms. It was drawn up by the United Nations Commissioner for Eritrea, a Bolivian, and is, as someone has aptly observed, "A Bolivian's idea of a Swiss Federation applied to Ethiopia." It is probably well, from the official Ethiopian point of view, that the Eritrean document is so little understood by the peoples of the Empire, for if thoroughly understood—and applied—it could well prove the focal point of a great deal of political unrest.

The territory of Eritrea has an area of some 50,000 square miles, about one-eighth the size of Ethiopia proper. The Ethiopian uplands project into Eritrea, forming the central Eritrean plateau, which varies in height from 6,000 to 8,000 feet and is in places very mountainous. The mountains become quite broken to the north and turn hilly in their descent to the Sudan. To the east they slope more steeply to the Red Sea plain and to the west more gradually to the Sudan plains. The climate is in general dry and warm, becoming very hot in the lowlands. Rainfall averages twenty inches annually over much of the highlands, but, as in Ethiopia, it is restricted to three or four months of the year. Elsewhere rainfall is inadequate for crops, except for a small area just north of Asmara, which gets upwards of forty inches a year. An intensely hot desert climate prevails in the Red Sea plains and in parts of the western lowlands, which are malarial in summer. Only one river in Eritrea flows for more than three months of the year, the Setit on the southern frontier with Ethiopia. Underground water is scarce. Less than 3 per cent of Eritrea's total area is estimated to be cultivable, 5 per cent is wooded, about 75 per cent serves as grazing land for the territory's estimated 3½ million livestock, and the rest is scrub or wasteland. Eritrea is clearly poor farming country. Since some four-fifths of the population are nevertheless dependent on farming as a livelihood, it does not take much to conclude that their standard of living must be very low, lower even than that of their Ethiopian neighbors to the south, who live on more fertile land.

Native farmers must also contend with a stony soil, often badly eroded as a result of severe deforestation and inadequate terracing and leveling. On the mountainsides there is generally no soil left, only bare rock, making afforestation difficult, the more so in view of the scarcity of water. Eritrean agriculture has other problems, too. There has always been a cereals deficit, which has been offset mostly by imports from Ethiopia. No remedy for this deficit is in sight. The acreage under cultivation cannot be increased without encroaching on already overstocked grazing land. In the eastern lowlands a moderate expansion is possible by flood irrigation, but in the western lowlands, where malaria exists, settlers are few. Furthermore, water is very scarce and irrigation would be partly at the expense of the dum palms lining the river banks, which provide the raw material for several manufacturing industries. Finally, the native system of land tenure, based on kinship groups, restricts the incentive to land improvement.

The Eritrean population was estimated at something under 1,100,000 in 1950. It consists of a mosaic of different groups, principally the Tigrinya-speaking Coptic highlanders, the nomadic Arab-Beja tribes of the western lowlands and the Red Sea plains, the Arab-Afar nomads occupying the coastal plains south of the Gulf of Zula, and the negroid agriculturalists of the extreme southwest. A fifth group consists of urbanized Eritreans living in Asmara, Massawa, and a few other towns.

These various population groups have different economic habits and different forms of social organization. Of the total rural population of some 850,000, no more than three-fifths are settled agriculturalists; the rest are nomads. Many different languages are spoken by the numerous tribes within these broad racial groupings. About half are Moslems, the remainder mainly Copts. Most are organized in kinship groups of families, claiming descent from a common ancestor. Among the settled agriculturalists, hereditary land right is often corporate and vested in these kinship groups.

Needless to say, the educational standard of all these people is very low. The Italians provided only elementary schooling for Eritreans during their occupation of the country, and in 1950, under British rule, only some 10,000 Eritrean children were attending school, about 6 per cent of the Eritrean population of school age.[4] Illiteracy is consequently very high.

Outside of agriculture and herding, the principal avenues of employment for Eritreans are manufacturing and mining, rail and road transportation, and public administration. Prior to federation with Ethiopia, less than 2 per cent of the native population of Eritrea were employed in all of these activities together.

The European population of Eritrea was small before the preparations for the Italian attack on Ethiopia in 1935, but increased rapidly thereafter. In 1941 the Italian population numbered some 60,000, with additional small Greek, Arab, Jewish, Indian, and Sudanese communities. By 1950 the number of Italians had declined to 20,000. In addition, there were then about 25,000 half-castes, of Italian father and Eritrean mother. The Italian community in Eritrea, much reduced today even below the 1950 level, still supplies most of the region's artisans, technicians, professional men, and entrepreneurs.

Since the federation with Ethiopia, the continued exodus of Italians from Eritrea has reduced economic activity in Asmara, the capital, to a very low level. The Eritreans do not require, and indeed cannot afford, the many and varied goods and services, both domestic and imported, which the city's former European inhabitants once enjoyed. Consequently, many shops have closed for lack of business and many houses and villas stand empty for rental at a low price. Other economic signs are more encouraging. A large military construction program undertaken by the U.S. Army at its Signal Corps base in Asmara has been helpful, and there has also been some new investment in industry since federation, notably in meat-packing and canning, in ceramics, and in cotton textiles. As yet, however, there has been no indication of a return to anything like the region's former level of commercial and industrial activity.

Eritrea's present-day manufacturing industry dates chiefly from 1936, when Italy launched a vast building and road construction program in newly conquered Ethiopia. In connection with this program

---

[4] This compares with perhaps 4 or 5 per cent in Ethiopia.

cement, brick, and tile factories were established in Eritrea and many servicing and electrical workshops were set up to cater to the transport fleet and the enlarged Italian population. "Many of the transport and construction works were no longer needed after the liberation of Ethiopia and the British occupation of Eritrea, and today, after the departure of 2/3 of the Italian civilians, rows of derelict buildings mark the scene in the smaller towns en route to Ethiopia, and in the partly demolished Italian and Allied military and naval bases."[5]

"In the few big towns, however, a new phase of industrial expansion set in after 1943. When the wartime shortages threw the territory back on its own supplies, Italian ingenuity and enterprise played an important role in improvising new factories, to make such consumer goods as bottles, glassware, matches, beer, wine, paper, and soap."[6] Other enterprises founded by the Italians and still in operation today turn out cereals, edible oils, vegetable fiber products, ceramics, furniture, dum-nut buttons, and fish meal. There are also electric power plants, salt works, flour mills, tanneries, a cotton factory, a cigarette factory, dry-cleaning plants, several meat factories, and other food-processing plants.

The sources of power for running Eritrea's factories have had to be mainly imported, since the low Eritrean rainfall and seasonal stream flow severely limit the possibility of local hydroelectric development. Eritrea produced in 1950 about 22.5 million kilowatt-hours of electricity, nine-tenths of which was generated from imported coal and oil. This is some two-thirds of the present-day public output in Ethiopia proper, illustrating again the greater relative degree of industrial development in Eritrea.

The Italians constructed a fairly complete road system for Eritrea,

[5] Report of the United Nations Commission for Eritrea, 1950, p. 14. The Eritreans reduced to ruin many of these abandoned Italian dwellings by removing window frames, doors, and roofs, and by building fires in the middle of the floor, as they were used to doing in their own huts. Similar destruction took place in Jimma, in southwestern Ethiopia, and in other Ethiopian towns where handsome Italian structures once stood.

[6] *Ibid.*

as well as a railway and ropeway from the port of Massawa to the capital of Asmara. The railway continues on beyond Asmara to Bisha, a distance of 224 miles in all. The Italian motor road system has been described by the United Nations Commission for Eritrea as an engineering feat. It comprises 485 miles of primary roads connecting all the important centers of Eritrea. In addition, there are some 1,400 miles of secondary roads and tracks. Responsibility for the maintenance of the primary road system has in recent years been assumed by the Imperial Highway Authority of Ethiopia.

Eritrea possesses two seaports, Massawa and Assab, through which now pass between 50 per cent and 60 per cent of the Empire's exports and imports. Massawa, the superior natural port and also the better developed of the two, serves mainly Eritrea and northern Ethiopia; Assab, farther south, is the port serving the central and southern portions of the country. A road originally constructed by the Italians and renovated by the Imperial Highway Authority connects the port with the towns of Dessie and Addis Ababa, and thence with the other parts of the country. Massawa, as already indicated, is connected both by rail and by road with the Eritrean and the Ethiopian hinterland.

Accurate data on the foreign trade of Eritrea are difficult to obtain for the period prior to federation, partly because some Ethiopian exports to Eritrea were always reprocessed and listed in the Eritrean trade statistics as native Eritrean produce. Such was the case with a great many hides and skins smuggled across the Ethiopian border into Eritrea. In the latter years of the British administration, 1947–49, total exports averaged £1,597,000 annually and total imports £3,220,000, leaving an average annual trade deficit of £1,623,000. However, Eritrea before federation had considerable "invisible" earnings from her transit trade with Ethiopia, from the value added to Ethiopian primary products re-sorted, cleaned, or processed in Eritrea for export, and from dollar remittances to American armed forces personnel, so that this adverse trade balance was largely wiped out. In the period mentioned, foreign receipts and payments were, in fact, in approximate balance. The principal exports of the country are agricultural, not industrial, chiefly hides, skins, salt, and marine products.

Before federation Eritrea's cereals deficit had to be made up by imports from Ethiopia. Textiles, fuels, and automotive parts were also important imports. Since federation there have been no separate trade statistics for Eritrea. With the continued exodus of Europeans, and their replacement to some extent by Eritreans and Ethiopians, the pattern of import demand in Eritrea has undoubtedly undergone a change, the more so since the higher Ethiopian customs tariff has considerably raised the price of imported articles in Eritrea. Probably there has been some decline in the volume of imports (including what was formerly imported from Ethiopia) as well, and to this extent the previously existing trade gap has been narrowed. In any case, it has been swallowed up in the trade surplus which the Empire as a whole has had with the rest of the world since 1950. It seems likely that Eritrea's "invisible" earnings, though now in her own currency (the Ethiopian dollar circulates in both countries), have continued substantially to redress the territory's adverse balance of trade, so that the support of Eritrea's population has not proved to be, as some feared, a heavily subsidized operation for Ethiopia.

Although the Federal Act provides that "Customs duties on goods entering or leaving the federation which have their final destination or origin in Eritrea shall be assigned to Eritrea" (para. 4), it has been impossible in practice to determine this proportion in view of the absence of customs barriers between the two countries. Consequently, a provisional agreement was reached between the Ethiopian and Eritrean authorities to pay a fixed amount of Eth.$1,156,890 per quarter to Eritrea as its share in customs duties.

Budgetary estimates for Eritrea covering the year 1947 E.C. (September 11, 1954, through September 10, 1955) indicate that Eritrean revenues and expenditures were each on the order of Eth.$11.5 million annually, and were approximately in balance. In the period indicated, some 40 per cent of the revenue was derived from customs duties. About one-sixth came from income taxes (which are higher in Eritrea than in Ethiopia), levied on the basis of an old Italian law amended under the British administration. Excise taxes and earnings on the state's tobacco and match monopoly contributed an almost equal amount. The balance was accounted for by miscellaneous smaller taxes (including land taxes, license fees, fines, and stamp duties) and other revenues.

Expenditures for police, medical services, and education were the three largest items on the outgo side of the Eritrean budget in 1947 E.C., accounting for close to half of the total.[7] Another 8½ per cent went for district (rural) administration. In addition, the Federal government was spending some Eth.$6.5 million in Eritrea in support of its various responsibilities there, including Eth.$2.7 million in partial subsidization of the unprofitable railway, and several smaller amounts for port administration, federal highways, postal services, customs collection, maintenance and expenses of the office of the Emperor's Representative in Eritrea, and other charges. These federal expenditures were financed, at least in part, by a federal surtax of 10 per cent on imports and of 2 per cent on exports, plus a federal tax on salt. To judge from verbal reports, these new levies do not offset in their entirety the federal expenditures in Eritrea, but the resulting deficit is not as large as had been anticipated even by the Ethiopian authorities prior to federation.

The most important economic effects of federation were the sharp rise in the cost of imports due to the higher Ethiopian customs tariff, which replaced the British rates; the rise in the cost of living which this entailed and the associated rise in labor costs, especially in urban centers; the loss of preferential Italian treatment for Eritrean exports; the partial compensation for this loss in the opening up of the Ethiopian market for Eritrean manufactures; and the change in the pattern of import demand resulting from the departure of Europeans. None of this had much effect on the population as a whole. Agriculture, the basic economic factor in Eritrea, was not and could not be affected by any of the political changes. It remains a subsistence agriculture, plagued by lack of water and by lack of cultivable land where there is water. Although no statistics are available, it seems plain that agricultural output has not greatly changed, except as

[7] Banditry, stemming from a variety of causes, continued to plague Eritrea after as before federation, requiring the expenditure of large sums for the maintenance of law and order.

regards the Italian farms previously producing for the urban market, and that the farmer's standard of living has not improved. Eritrea, not being a producer of coffee, has not shared in the coffee boom.

The United Nations Commission which investigated the political sentiments of the Eritrean people in 1950 concluded that a majority of them probably favored political association with Ethiopia, but noted that a large minority (mainly among the Moslems of the western province and in the Red Sea division, including the Danakil desert) opposed the change. A reconciliation of these opposing views was attempted in the federal solution for the territory. How has this solution, so foreign to the strongly centralist tradition of the Ethiopian State, worked out?

It is difficult to say. There has been a conspicuous lack of publicity on the subject, stemming in part from the low level of general political interest (particularly in Ethiopia), in part from the almost complete absence of public discussion, and in part from the invisible hand of censorship, which gives the press to understand that the mention of anything political is taboo. There was at first some public interest and newspaper comment in Eritrea, but the newspapers there were soon cowed when the Emperor's Representative in Eritrea attacked one of them that dared to speak out too openly. Although the Eritrean courts did not act against the offender, no further instances of outspokenness have occurred. Freedom of the press and other communications media is guaranteed by the Eritrean constituition, as it now is also by the constitution of Ethiopia, but traditional inhibitions are strong.

Apart from isolated instances, there seem to have been no great pressures by either government, on the one hand to assert the considerable powers of an independent, freely elected, democratic Eritrean government or, on the other, to swallow up Eritrea in the Ethiopean Empire by effectively undermining its local political autonomy.[8] The Eritreans, financially weak and dependent on the Federal government for development expenditures, have acquiesced in whatever the Ethiopians have proposed, while the latter, lacking the ad-

---

[8] Recall, however, the labor-code incident of October 1957 (p. 118).

ministrative capacity and the determination to go much farther, have hesitated to follow up their advantage. Their approach to Eritrean affairs has been extremely paternalistic, but not dictatorial, and they have refrained from coercion. Many of their actions, particularly in health and education—matters supposedly under the exclusive internal jurisdiction of Eritrea—have been high-handed and have smacked of interference. In reply to criticism from members of the Eritrean Assembly that the Federal government had usurped the wealth and violated the rights of Eritrea by intervening in Eritrean internal affairs, the Emperor's Representative to Eritrea, Bitwoded Andargatchew Massai, stated in 1955 that "there are no internal nor external affairs as far as the office of His Imperial Majesty's Representative is concerned, and there will be none in the future. The affairs of Eritrea concern Ethiopia as a whole and the Emperor."[9]

The Eritreans, for their part, have not pressed the issue and have been content to let things drift. In any case, there have been few further reports of criticism or of interference in Eritrean internal affairs. The explanation seems to be that the Eritreans are not sufficiently aware of what federation really means, nor sufficiently mature to assert their political rights in an effort to safeguard and strengthen by use the substantial democratic freedoms guaranteed them by their constitution and backed by United Nations prestige. It seems all too likely that the future will see a gradual withering of the spirit of independent government in Eritrea and the ultimate domination, if not absorption, of that government by Ethiopian centralism.

[9] Speech delivered on the opening of the first regular session of the Eritrean Assembly, March 28, 1955.

XI

Conclusion

In the foregoing chapters an attempt has been made to present a sort of bird's-eye view of the Empire of Ethiopia, or Abyssinia, as it was formerly known. In this attempt an unavoidable emphasis has been laid on the economic side of the picture, partly because the author's experience of the country has been primarily in this sphere, but also because it is mainly at this point of her national life that Ethiopia has had the greatest degree of contact with the modern world. The large postwar expansion of the country's foreign trade alone has multiplied such contacts enormously. By far the main concern of foreigners in Ethiopia is with this trade, or some aspect of it, and of course the interest of foreign investors in Ethiopia is similarly commercial or economic. Even the Point Four program has chiefly economic aims and produces chiefly economic results. And the most important reforming measures undertaken by the Ethiopian government since the restoration have been economic or fiscal in nature.

There is no question, in fact, that the economic impact of the growth of trade, of foreign investment, of road improvement, and of monetary and fiscal reform has done more to change the face of Ethiopia in the last fifteen years than the combined influence of all other factors prior to that time, the Italian occupation and the construction of the Djibouti-Addis Ababa railroad possibly excepted.

There is also no question that a great deal more remains to be accomplished before Ethiopia can rank herself among the civilized nations of the world. Changes of the kind required to convert a primitive, heterogeneous, tradition-bound people into a modern, unified nation cannot possibly take place in a few years. Even in the Soviet Union, where the initial base of achievement was incomparably higher, it has required the most ruthless dictatorship and single-mind-edness of aim and action to bring about significant results within the span of one generation. Japan, where the level of economic activity one hundred years ago was perhaps not far from that of Ethiopia today, took over two generations to "modernize." No such spectacular results need be looked for in Ethiopia. The monarchy, though abso-lute, is not ruthless or fanatical, or particularly displeased with the economic status quo. The people, by and large, are content with their lot. Above all, there is the Ethiopian character, with its shortcomings in the way of resourcefulness and initiative. It is surprising how im-portant intangible qualities of character can be in influencing the shape and pace of economic progress, but this has been demonstrated again and again, most recently in postwar Germany.

The availability of capital is of secondary importance. Capital and the will to use it must go hand in hand; neither is sufficient by and of itself. Capital can be created; the will to use it is either there or not there. In Ethiopia, as in other underdeveloped countries, special lending institutions have been set up to advance funds to small bor-rowers on very easy terms. No one has yet been trampled in the rush to apply for such funds. Private investors have found that it does not pay to erect huge factories where there is no effective market to buy up their production. There must be a "balanced growth," to use Nurkse's phrase, if such investment is to be profitable and is to initiate a cumulative economic advance. There must also be a strong acquisi-tive desire on the part of the people and the purchasing power to make that desire effective. These factors, in turn, depend on others that have their roots in the state and organization of society and the be-liefs, ideals, and values of the people who compose it. In primitive societies the more sophisticated economic motivations do not exist, and the mere availability of capital means little or nothing.

In Ethiopia these points must be emphasized. The economic growth that has taken place there in the most recent period has not been internally generated but has been mainly the result of fortuitous external factors, among them the heavy Italian capital investment in 1936–41, the large postwar influx of foreigners, and the advantageous rise in agricultural prices, particularly the price of coffee. Internally, this expansion has been assisted by the adoption of a national monetary unit and fiscal reform. But elsewhere the government has paid mere lip service to the ideal of economic development. Almost all the initiative has come from foreign sources.

Ethiopia remains a nation of farmers and herdsmen, producing largely on a subsistence basis and almost incidentally for export. It has only lately rid itself of a semifeudal economic and social system based on serfdom and slavery, and the mentality associated with these institutions still remains—the emphasis on rank and status, tribal and provincial loyalties. The mass of the people are ignorant of the larger world beyond the bounds of their immediate experience, and are satisfied to go on living as their ancestors lived for centuries. The progress made since the end of the war is visible mainly in the sphere of foreign trade and in a few urban centers.

It is extremely unfortunate for the country that adulation of the Emperor and the imperial prerogatives exerts such a stranglehold on responsible administration at lower levels of government. As a result of this adulation and the encouragement it gives to seek advancement through the royal favor, one of the main concerns of Ethiopian government officials from the ministers on down is to secure their own position and to undermine that of others by a practice of intrigue and denunciation. Fear of incurring displeasure among superiors is too often the guiding motivation of subordinate employees. As long as the influence of monarchy is so pervasive in Ethiopia, there seems little hope for the development of responsible democratic government. The revised constitution notwithstanding, Parliament will remain a dead letter and the independence of the judiciary a vain illusion. The implementation of civil rights and of free political expression will remain just fond hopes for the future.

On the positive side, however, it may be said that Ethiopia can count herself fortunate to have in Haile Selassie a ruler who is enlightened and desirous of furthering the material and spiritual progress of his country within the bounds of tradition and practicality. Although sometimes hoodwinked, he is one of the few Ethiopians with imagination and vision, and it is largely on his initiative that new projects or administrative reforms are carried out by the government. His command to execute a specific action seems to cut through the worst snarls of red tape. But the practical limitations on his ability to run the government single-handed are obvious. Too often where he does not, or cannot, take an immediate hand in affairs the business of government languishes. The power and uniqueness of his position at the head of the Ethiopian government are the cause both of nothing's being done and of something's getting done at all.

In the field of foreign affairs Ethiopia has taken an active part since the restoration of the monarchy in 1941. Even before the Italian invasion of 1935 Ethiopia had been a member of the League of Nations. Her unfortunate experience with this body, which refused to come to her aid when she was attacked, seems not to have dissuaded the Emperor from the conviction that foreign attachments are worth while. Ethiopia is a founding member of the United Nations as well as of the International Monetary Fund and the International Bank for Reconstruction and Development. She has received help from all of these organizations in the postwar period and has sent delegations to numerous international conferences. She has had a growing amount of foreign financial aid and private foreign investment, and has received some U.S.$16 million in long-overdue Italian war reparations (three-fourths of which will go for the Koka dam project). The Emperor is a fervent supporter of the doctrine of collective security, to which he gave practical demonstration by sending a contingent of Ethiopian troops to Korea. As already indicated, Ethiopia has welcomed United States Point Four aid and has received technicians from FAO, WHO, and UNICEF. Foreign diplomatic representation in Ethiopia has greatly increased—evidence of the growing importance which this formerly little-known kingdom is assuming in the eyes of foreign powers. Many more foreigners are now in Ethiopia than at any time prior to the Italian invasion and occupation, and there are also more Ethiopian nationals abroad, mostly as students. Clearly the Emperor believes that the period of the country's long isolation from the rest of the world is over, and that Ethiopia must move forward and progress if she is not to slip back into obscurity. Unfortunately, such progress cannot be brought about by one man alone, though he be the Emperor. The pace at which Ethiopia develops will depend to a considerable extent on the degree to which the convictions, ideals, energy, and imagination that motivate this man can be transmitted to his people.

Index

Abbai, *see* Blue Nile

Abebe Aragai, 21

Abuna, *see* Archbishop

Addis Ababa: not representative of Ethiopia, 1; founded, 7, 18; fled by Emperor (1936), 21; re-entered (1941), 21; University College of, 27; municipal elections in, 54; mentioned, 24, 43, 47, 60, 97

Adola, 135

Adowa, battle of, 17, 18

Afa Negus, 45

African Rift, 3; *see also* Rift Valley

Agricultural and Commercial Bank of Ethiopia, 87, 129

Agriculture, 71–88; per cent of budget devoted to, 64; in Eritrea, 139–40

Agau, 9

Air Force, Ethiopian, 56–57

Air transportation, and Export-Import Bank loan, 123–24

Aksum, Kingdom of, 10, 11, 12, 25, 41

Alexandria, visited by Frumentius, 11

Alvarez, Father Francisco, 13

Ambas, 2, 14

Amharas: regions inhabited by, 24; Christianity of, 25; attitude toward physical labor, 64, 71

Anglo-Ethiopian Agreements, 22; and Ethiopian currency reform, 105

Ankober, 26

Archbishop of Ethiopia, 19, 33

Area: of Ethiopian Empire, 1; of Eritrea, 139

Army, Ethiopian, 55–57

Arogee, 16

Arts and sciences: literature stimulated by Solomonian restoration, 12; Ethiopia's contributions to, 36

Arussi, forests of, 7

Asmara, 97, 137–47 *passim*

Assab: bought by Italy, 17; loan for harbor improvement of, 67; value of imports handled by, 127

Awash River: and Rift Valley, 3; terminus of, 4; and Koka Dam, 120; mentioned, 72, 134

Balabats, 53, 55

Balance of payments: surplus of, 102, 103, 114; in Eritrea, 143–44

Banco di Roma, 98

Bandits: attacks on road camps, 126; in Eritrea, 145 n.

Bank deposits: expansion of, 101; of government with central bank, 102–3

Bank of Abyssinia, 98

Banque de l'Indo-Chine, 99

Barclay's Bank (D.C. & O.), 98, 99

Barka and Baro rivers, 7

Barter, 96, 104

Bisha, 122, 143

Black Jews, *see* Falashas

Blowers, George, 105

Blue Nile, 5, 7, 18, 24, 134 n.

British Military Mission to Ethiopia, 55–56

British subsidy (1942), 65

Bruce, James, 15

Budget: description of, 62–63; policy criticized, 63–65; extraordinary revenue, 65–67, 68; extraordinary expenditure, 69; of Eritrea, 144–45

Buxton, David, 2

Capital: invested in commerce, 95–96; in industry, 115; secondary importance of, 149

Cattle, 62, 84–85, 94

Central bank, *see* State Bank of Ethiopia

This book may be kept

FOURTEEN DAYS

A fine will be charged for each day the book
is kept over time.

DEC 12 '83			
APR 11 1985			
DEC 12 1988			
Harrow			
NOV 10 2009			